LOOK WHO'S TALKING!

LOOK WHO'S TALKING!

HOW TO HELP CHILDREN WITH THEIR COMMUNICATION SKILLS

ALISON MULVANEY

SIMON & SCHUSTER
AUSTRALIA

This book is dedicated to Robert Bellamy for his warmth, love and unending support.

AUTHOR'S NOTE

The incidence of communication handicap is much greater in males than females. It is for this reason, and for ease of expression, that I have chosen to use the male pronoun throughout when referring to a child with communication difficulties. Most speech pathologists are women, hence the female pronoun for referring to the professionals who work to help the children.

LOOK WHO'S TALKING!
First published in Australasia in 1991 by
Simon & Schuster Australia
20 Barcoo Street, East Roseville NSW 2069

A Paramount Communications Company
Sydney New York London Toronto Tokyo Singapore

© Alison Mulvaney 1991

National Library of Australia
Cataloguing in Publication data

Mulvaney, Alison.
   Look who's talking!: how to help children with their
   communication skills.

   Bibliography.
   Includes index.
   ISBN 0 7318 0235 7.

   1. Children — Language. 2. Oral communication — Study
   and teaching. I. Title

302.2242

Designed by Kumar Pereira

Typeset in Australia by Adtype Graphics Pty Ltd
Printed in Australia by Globe Press

Contents

PREFACE

Over the past ten years awareness of the incidence of communication handicap in our community has dramatically increased. People have also become more aware of communication and its importance in every aspect of daily living. As a result, the specialists dealing with communication difficulties — speech pathologists — have been faced with a huge increase in the number of children and adults whose communication skills need to be assessed and treated. This has created lengthy waiting lists and a great deal of frustration for both patients and speech pathologists.

It was out of my personal frustration with waiting lists that this book emerged — to offer some help to those parents in need.

This is not an academic book full of medical jargon but a practical manual on the more important aspects of communication. It has been written in an easy-to-read style and is full of practical hints.

You have probably at some time worried about your child's talking. Is he saying all the words he should? Are the words clear enough? Should you read to him more? If you are like many of the parents that I deal with, you either have a child receiving speech therapy, are on a waiting list somewhere for your child to receive speech therapy, or you just want to know if your child is functioning normally for his age.

This book is for you to use in a variety of ways. You can use it to learn what is normal speech development and what is not. You can use it to assess your child's communication skills and to learn more about communication problems and their effect on children and their families. It can be used to perform home treatment in the absence of a speech pathologist and also as an adjunct to speech therapy sessions. I strongly recommend, however, that if you believe your child has a communication problem you do seek professional help. Early intervention is the key to successful treatment.

While this book has been primarily written for parents, it is also for the family doctor, teachers, all caregivers, community health nurses and other health professionals. Many more children would obtain the help they need if professionals working with children knew when to refer a child with a possible communication problem. I hope that this book fills the gap, and provides an insight into the problems faced by the parents of children with communication difficulties.

At the very least I hope that it will serve as a source of hope for all parents. It will assure you that you are not alone in your concern for 'good talking' from your child, and will show you that working with your child can be both rewarding and great fun.

Chapter One

COMMUNICATION AND WHY PARENTS WORRY

All parents worry about their children. They worry about whether to breastfeed or bottlefeed, whether to use cloth nappies or disposables, whether to smack or pacify, whether their expectations are fair, and whether to send their child to a coeducational or single sex school.

Nothing seems to worry a parent more than their child's talking ability. First they worry about when he'll start talking, then they worry about not being able to understand him, then they worry when he starts to repeat the same word over and over. They wonder why he can't say certain sounds and why his sentences are back-to-front.

Parents also want to know what sort of help they can give their child at home. Whether or not they should tell the preschool or school teacher that there's a problem and whether they have caused the problem in any way. They also ask: Is it hereditary? Where can we go for help? What is speech therapy? What does it involve? Is there homework given? What will the treatment cost? How long will we have to wait before our child can start treatment? The list of questions goes on and on.

It is no small wonder that parents worry about their child's ability to communicate. Communication — the ability to listen, understand, speak, read, and write — is a basic and essential part of life. Good communication skills are needed to form and maintain relationships with other people, to pass effectively through any education system, and to gain and maintain a job.

Many children who have problems saying sounds or putting a sentence together become so frustrated that they develop poor and sometimes aggressive behaviour. Other children with such difficulties, or those who stutter, may withdraw from all social situations or even stop talking altogether. Almost all children who have difficulty communicating find the social and/or academic demands of school very trying.

Adolescents and adults with communication difficulties often struggle with embarrassment and find it stressful when having to perform in situations such as job interviews.

Once they have a job, they may go to great lengths to hide their limitations in reading, spelling, writing or even talking. Surely no parent would wish this upon their child. All parents want to provide their child with the best possible foundation for a happy, successful and rewarding future. Normal communication skills provide the cornerstone for such a future.

What is communication and how can it go wrong?

In its simplest form, communication is the giving and receiving of information. However, if we start to break down 'communication' into its many different components, we start to see that it's far from simple.

To be able to receive information a child has to be able to understand the message. To give information he has to be able to use the right sounds and put them together in a way the receiver will understand. Let's take each of these skills in turn and look at some of the common problem areas that children have to face.

To communicate effectively a child first has to be able to hear

the message given. For some children a hearing loss is the cause of their communication difficulties. Others who have normal hearing may have problems distinguishing one sound from another. For example, a child may not be able to hear the difference between the sounds /s/ and /sh/, even though he has normal hearing skills. He may confuse words such as 'sure' and 'sore'.

The second step in communicating is the ability to understand the message that you've been given. Children who know the meaning of only a limited number of words, or who have a poor understanding of grammar, may have great difficulty in understanding information or instructions given to them.

Some children have short memories and so can't hold a message in their minds long enough to interpret it. Instead they may only receive part of the message. As an example, take the little girl whose mother says: 'Feed the cat, put on your green jumper and meet me at the front door'. Unable to remember all these instructions, she may even forget whole portions of what she was asked to do, or she may mix up the instructions so that she puts the cat at the front door, puts on her red jumper and then opens the door of the fridge.

Clearly a child needs to be able to retain the message long enough to interpret it and then send a message back, thus completing the cycle of communication.

To send a message we need to effectively use all the sounds in our language. Many children leave off the first or last sounds in words, substitute one sound for another, for example 'tat' for 'cat', or distort a sound in a word. Any of these problems makes it difficult for others to understand what they are saying.

Voice abnormalities such as talking in too high or too low a voice, or talking with a harsh, hoarse voice can make it difficult for others to carry on a conversation with someone. These types of voice problems occur in young children.

Stuttering can also make it difficult for a child to return a message or to ask a question in class. Many school-aged stutterers are thought by their teachers to be poor participants in class because they don't put up their hands to ask or answer questions. This is because they are scared that they will stutter. Adolescent stutterers also often have difficulty obtaining and holding down a job as all jobs require some ability to communicate.

The ability to form an accurate sentence using the correct words, in the right order, with the correct meaning, is vital. Children develop the majority of sentence-forming skills by the time they are five years of age. Incorrect use of grammar, word order or sentence meaning between the ages of three and five may indicate that there is a language problem.

These are some of the areas of difficulty that children may face. To understand the significance of these problems we need to understand just how they can affect a child.

How will a communication problem affect my child?

There will be many people who will say that what you are about to read is an exaggerated picture of what really happens. For those of you who have a child with a communication problem please tell them *they are wrong*! A child with a communication problem has a great deal to cope with every day. It is best for parents to know what is in store for them from the beginning so that they can cope appropriately.

Perhaps the most effective way of illustrating how a significant 'talking problem' can affect a child is to describe some typical cases. The following descriptions are composites drawn from a large number of children.

Let me first tell you about Jonathan. Jonathan was three-and-a-half when I first saw him. He had a toothless grin and an even cheekier personality. He refused to talk with me or cooperate. Jonathan was a speech pathologist's nightmare dressed up in angel's overalls. His mother couldn't control his behaviour and he threw tantrums at the drop of a hat (usually in large department stores or busy medical centre waiting rooms).

Jonathan's talking consisted of a few isolated vowels such as /ah/, /oo/ and /oh/ and he relied heavily on hand gestures to communicate. He spent a good deal of time dragging his mother from one place to another so that she could find or get something for him — dragging her around was much easier for him than trying to say 'look'.

Jonathan understood everything that was said to him and his hearing was perfect. His longest sentence, however, consisted of two words together which sounded like 'ee oo' but meant 'me too'.

Here was a very frustrated little boy who was having a great deal of difficulty in getting his message across. Instead of being referred to a speech pathologist, his mother had been ridiculed for being neurotic and over-protective.

Now let's look at Annie. Annie was five and although an out-going child at home, was like a frightened rabbit when in public. There were tears each morning as she went off to school. School wasn't much fun for Annie as the other children either ignored her when she talked, or teased her by copying the way she talked. When visitors dropped in for a chat with her parents,

Annie refused to utter a word and hid behind her mother, or ran off to her bedroom.

Annie had an articulation disorder: a problem in saying some sounds. Her speech was unclear and in long sentences sounded slurred. Strangers couldn't understand her and neither could her father. Annie didn't receive help until she was four years old. A full year of weekly visits to the speech pathologist made a terrific difference, but there was still a long way to go.

Simon was nine years old and bottom of the class. He couldn't understand what his mother was saying when she gave him detailed instructions. Simon didn't know his left from his right, he didn't know the days of the week or the months of the year, he didn't know the opposites of words and he had great difficulty in spelling simple words.

Simon's mother had approached his teacher many times and had even arranged meetings with the principal. She was told that Simon clowned around in class, was disruptive, never completed his work and couldn't sit still. He had a learning difficulty and a personality to match. His behaviour was immature and he would often say or do inappropriate things, but sometimes he would make quirky little comments that made his father think he was a genius. Simon had many years of school to get through and very few skills to help him along the way.

Marcus was four years old when he was referred for a problem with pronunciation of the sound /s/. Saying this sound properly, however, turned out to be the least of his worries. Marcus had an expressive language problem. He used long sentences which made his parents think that his talking was normal, but he didn't use any of the grammatical structures that a four-year-old should use. Instead Marcus talked like a three-year-old. It took his parents some time to understand that he had a language problem, and that it wouldn't correct itself when he started school.

Marcus had to be taught rules for the parts of grammar that he didn't have in his sentences, and had to be taught how and when to use these grammatical structures. A complex problem indeed, but one that could be fixed through regular treatment.

Natalie was six and almost as quiet as Annie. She had a severe stutter characterised by her repeating words, and parts of words, over and over again. She would avoid saying certain words for fear of stuttering on them and she blinked her eyes when she stuttered, making her look even more uncomfortable. Natalie avoided talking as much as possible and was clearly embarrassed by her problem. Her father also stuttered and was determined that Natalie should have the help that he had so desperately needed as a child but never received. He was concerned that she would be teased at school, and early into the first grade this became a reality. Natalie, however, responded very quickly to treatment and within a month she had her stuttering under control. She became more outgoing and was no longer teased at school.

Walk into the playground at Matthew's preschool and you could hear him shouting at the top of his voice. Walk into his backyard after preschool when his two older brothers came home to play and you could hear him screeching even louder. Matthew was doing something that is very easily done by us all, he was abusing his voice. This continuous abuse of the vocal cords was beginning to damage them. When Matthew was talking his voice sounded harsh and hoarse. He was prone to short bouts of laryngitis and by the age of four had lost his voice completely on two occasions. Matthew's parents hadn't realised that he had a problem until the preschool teacher mentioned it. It was a voice disorder that could easily be fixed. Voice therapy with a speech pathologist prevented Matthew from having to have surgery on his vocal cords (and his older brothers stopped screaming too).

Nathan was two years of age and saying very little. He babbled and jargoned (played around making sounds) constantly but would never say a real word. The frustrating thing was that Nathan could show his mother he understood everything she said to him. She kept on wondering why he wouldn't talk. By this stage he should have had a large number of single words in his vocabulary and a number of two-word sentences like 'dad car' under his belt. A speech pathologist taught Nathan's mother how to stimulate his language and how to change their home environment to make him want to talk. Within five weeks he spoke his first single words and from then on there was no holding him back.

These cases illustrate just some of the problems that children may have with their communication. Many children can have a combination of two or three of these problems, at varying degrees of severity. It is common, for example, for a child to suffer from both a language comprehension problem and an expressive language problem. It is also not uncommon for there to be an articulation difficulty associated with both of these. Every child will be different.

How will my family be affected?

The social, emotional and financial affairs of a family can be dramatically affected by the communication handicap of one family member. All members of the family are likely to experience a degree of stress, but from my experience it seems to be the mother that bears the greatest burden.

In many cases, a mother may have a strong feeling that there is something wrong with her child's talking, but will not seek help because maybe the family doctor has said 'Don't worry about it. My own child didn't talk until he was three,' or her husband insists that there's nothing wrong. But delaying assessment and diagnosis of a handicap is a recipe for greater stress. It is far better to know the facts and deal with them than to have the worry of 'what ifs'.

Receiving a diagnosis that there actually is a problem will, of course, be disturbing, but recognising a problem is the first step towards solving it.

Many parents suffer from varying degrees of guilt once it has been established that their child has a communication problem. They feel that they couldn't have spent enough time with the child, didn't read to him enough or were negligent in any number of other ways. The fact is, however, that a parent is rarely identified as the cause of the problem. It is only in extreme cases of stimulus deprivation, drug taking or child abuse that a direct relationship between the parents and the problem can be identified.

Genetic inheritance plays a part in some disorders, such as stuttering and learning difficulties, but in no way could a parent blame themselves for their child having such a problem.

Many parents deny that any problem exists. This seems to be the case more with fathers than with mothers, from my experience. Once they work through the denial and come to a point where they can accept the given circumstances they can then begin to provide their child with the help that he needs.

Sometimes other professionals, particularly general practitioners, bear the brunt of a parent's anger. They are accused of failing to refer the child for help when the parents first became concerned. Thankfully, due to an increased awareness by the medical profession of communication problems and their effects on the individual and his family, more and more children are being referred in good time to speech pathologists.

Parents often feel tremendously frustrated and helpless once they discover that their child has a communication problem. Such feelings can be fuelled by relatives who are sure that 'he didn't get it from our side of the family'. Confusion can also arise through people offering all sorts of conflicting advice. It is best to ignore the next door neighbour's guidance, whether he or she is a teacher, nurse, doctor or preacher, and seek professional advice from a speech pathologist. If you find you have to wait for help, this book will be of assistance.

Another source of stress may be the financial burden of private treatment. I have known many mothers who, because they want their child to have private treatment, have returned to the workforce to pay for it.

But I have been encouraged to see, over the years, more and more fathers bringing their children for speech pathology assessment. An increasing number of fathers, too, are asking to be included in the homework activities and it is frequently they who bring their children in for regular treatment sessions. This is a very positive step forward for both parents. It helps to relieve the pressure upon the mother, and allows the father to be closely involved in the remediation procedure. Working together can strengthen the marriage and the family unit, with each member taking their share of responsibility for the family situation.

Siblings can often be adversely affected by the communication problem of a brother or sister. It is easy for parents to devote so much of their attention to the child who has difficulties and to lavish so much money on him, that the other children in the family feel left out. Parents must guard against this occurring.

If your child has an obvious problem, you are likely to come across people you don't know who just have to point out that he is not speaking properly. My advice is to take a deep breath, thank them for their advice and then move away as soon as possible. You need to keep a positive frame of mind, and the last thing you should allow to get you down is the well-meaning busybody.

If your child's problem is a severe one, you may be faced with his frustration being directed squarely at you. Many children with severe communication problems also have some behavioural problems. Try to stay calm and patient. Try to see the child's point of view, but at the same time let him know that his behaviour is unacceptable. See Chapter 10 for more help in dealing with this particular problem.

A child's communication problem can affect the parents' relationship, sometimes strengthening it, sometimes pulling it apart. By maintaining a realistic outlook, sharing all responsibilities, making sure you have time alone together, keeping the lines of communication open, and seeking professional counselling when needed, there is every chance that your relationship with your partner, and with your children, will grow stronger rather than weaker.

Reading about all of these problems may leave you feeling a little overwhelmed, but it is best to be aware of the possible hardships from the outset. Don't be discouraged. Dwell on the positive and remember even if you are waiting for professional help, you can do something to help your child if you follow the advice in this book.

When and how to seek help for your child

Below is a simple guide to follow if you are worried about a child's communication skills and wondering whether or not to seek professional help. While age limits are approximate, I have placed them at what is generally considered to be the upper age limits for developing a skill.

Refer the child for a speech pathology assessment if:

- The parents or other family members are worried.
- The child is eighteen months old and doesn't have a range of single words and/or didn't play with sounds much as a baby.
- The child is two years old and is not using two-word sentences.
- The child is three years old and is not easily understood by others.
- The child is four-and-a-half and his sentence structure and use of grammar are poor.
- The child is five-and-a-half and still has difficulty saying the following sounds: /s, z, r, l, v, j/.
- The child has difficulty understanding others.
- The child is frustrated by his inability to talk properly.
- The child has hesitations in his speech.
- The child has a husky, breathy or nasal voice, or has continual bouts of laryngitis.

- The child has significant difficulties in reading, mathematics, spelling or writing.
- The child appears to be unable to follow instructions that are lengthy or complex.

When it comes to seeking help for a communication problem my advice is try all available resources without delay. Your first step should be to contact your paediatrician, baby health clinic sister, or family doctor. These professionals will probably direct you towards the major hospital or local health centre in your area, both of which should offer speech pathology services. Speech pathologists deal with the diagnosis and treatment of *all* communication problems.

If you contact either of these facilities your child may be placed on a waiting list. It is important that you ask exactly on what list your child has been placed. Don't assume that if his name is on a list he will receive treatment as soon as you are called. At many facilities there are two lists: an assessment waiting list and a treatment waiting list. If you have already been given a speech pathology assessment at another facility, then your child's name may be placed directly on the treatment waiting list.

If, like many parents, you find that the waiting lists are six months or more long, and you're not prepared to wait for help, you can ask the hospital to give you the names of private speech pathologists in your area. They, too, may have waiting lists, but they are seldom long.

No matter what your course of action, the answer to 'When should I seek help for my child?' is *now*. The earlier the intervention, the better the prognosis. Too many children are referred for help just before starting school. By this time they have had almost five years in which to set up abnormal communication patterns. Once they are at school they may have difficulties socially and academically, and indeed may have to miss important parts of school to attend their therapy sessions with the speech pathologist. Of course every parent would like their child to receive treatment out of school hours, but this is not always possible.

Remember that you, as a parent, usually know if there is really something wrong with your child. Follow your instincts. This is the best advice I can give any parent. Early intervention could mean that your child's problem will be resolved well before starting school.

What does a speech pathologist do?

The term speech pathology literally means 'speech abnormality', which is, in fact, a truly inadequate description of what speech pathologists can do.

A speech pathologist will usually start an assessment by taking a detailed history of your child's birth, medical details, fine and gross motor skills development and his speech development. She will also ask whether there is a history of communication problems in the family and if your child has had speech pathology treatment before.

The next step is for the pathologist to assess your child's communication skills. She will check his ability to articulate sounds. She will also check the structure and function of your child's teeth, lips, tongue and hard and soft palates to ensure that there are no physiological abnormalities affecting his ability to produce sounds.

Speech pathologists use both structured tests and informal observation to check voice and fluency, and to determine whether your child's ability to understand, retain and express language is normal for his age. They are also qualified to assess specific symptoms of learning difficulties.

As you can see, speech pathologists can assess, diagnose and treat every aspect of communication skills.

Causes and cures

There are times when the cause of a communication problem is obvious. The child may have been born with structural damage to the mouth such as a cleft palate, or damage to the nervous system such as occurs with cerebral palsy. The child may be deaf, intellectually handicapped or autistic.

Much of the time, however, causes can be found, but they are less obvious. For example, the child may have spent a great deal of time in and out of hospital during the first five years of his life and this may have interrupted his development; there may be a strong history of delayed speech and language development in the family and a number of relatives may also have children with communication problems; the child may have suffered numerous ear infections over the years which may have interfered sufficiently with his hearing to cause a problem in development. The list goes on and on.

Sometimes it may be impossible to pin-point the cause. Coming to terms with this can be difficult for parents, and they may go from one professional to another in the hope that someone will provide them with an answer.

But no matter what has caused the child's difficulties, treatment is the crucial factor. Parents should not worry so much about the cause, but rather focus upon the cure for the sake of the child.

All speech pathologists use similar methods of treatment. Although the length of treatment sessions may vary, most treatment sessions occur on a weekly basis. You will probably find that you will be encouraged to join in the sessions if the child is cooperative, and nine times out of ten you will be given follow-up work to do at home. It may take you a little time before you can establish a regular routine for speech therapy homework. You may need to set a regular time and place each day, and make it clear to other family members that this is your time with your child and there are to be no interruptions. Sometimes older brothers and sisters can be involved in the homework, but I would warn you against allowing siblings to correct your child's speech or language as this can cause major problems. You can have them help by cutting out pictures and pasting them in the speech therapy workbook or involve them in the language games. Most speech pathologists will record exactly what you need to do for homework in the child's speech therapy workbook, and will demonstrate the work for you in case you have any problems once you get home.

Once a child's communication problem has been overcome, the treatment program is usually stopped and an appointment made for a review assessment. At the review appointment, the therapist will decide whether there is any need for further intervention. If the child's communication skills are within normal limits for his age, then the child will not need further treatment. The parent is, of course, encouraged to contact the therapist if any further problems arise.

There are a wide variety of treatment techniques for all communication disorders and because there is always new knowledge emerging speech pathology is a rapidly changing and advancing profession. Parents should feel entirely confident that their child will receive the treatment he needs.

KEY POINTS

- To communicate effectively a child has to be able to:
  hear the message
  distinguish the sounds
  retain the message long enough to interpret it
  understand the message
  correctly use sounds and grammar to send or return a message.
- A child with a communication problem has a great deal to cope with and it can adversely affect his behaviour.
- Recognising that a child has a communication problem is the first step towards solving it.
- Seek professional advice immediately if you are worried.
- Early intervention is the key to solving the problem.
- The cause of a communication problem may be difficult to establish.
- Speech pathology usually involves weekly sessions with the pathologist and regular work at home.

Chapter Two

THE NORMAL DEVELOPMENT OF COMMUNICATION SKILLS

Most people believe that children start to speak automatically and without any trouble at all; and many children do. The acquisition of language, however, is a very complicated matter indeed, extensively studied but not yet completely understood.

The development of a child's communication skills happens across two areas: articulation and language. It is often difficult to separate these two areas as the development of both coincides so closely, especially up to about the age of eighteen months.

Articulation is the word used to describe the production of speech sounds, that is, vowels and consonants (see Chapter 6 for a detailed explanation of articulation and the production of speech). By the age of about eighteen months a child's articulation skills are usually sufficiently developed for an assessment to be made as to whether there might be problems in this area.

Just what is language? To fully describe such a complex process would be a major undertaking. The simplified explanation that follows will provide a reasonable background against which you can understand more about your child's language development.

Language can be broken down into two parts: competence, what we know; and performance, how we use our knowledge.

Gaining competence is not a conscious process. We learn the rules of language without anyone teaching them to us and without us even being aware that we are learning them. Competence comes before performance, that is, we know the rules of our language in order to use them for communication.

When we learn a language we learn the sounds used in the

language, the basic units of meaning (words) and we learn the rules for combining these words to form sentences and for combining many sentences. These elements and rules of our language are referred to as the grammar. The grammar is what we know — it represents our competence — and it is shared, so that we can talk to and understand each other.

Grammar can basically be divided up into four components: the sound system; the rules of word formation; the rules of sentence formation; and the system of meaning.

A baby is learning language from the moment it is born. Let's now look more closely at how language develops from birth to five years of age.

Although children have an inborn capacity to develop communication skills, they must be provided with stimulation to encourage normal development. Putting a child in a playpen for 24 hours and leaving him to his own devices is asking for trouble. Children need to be talked to and listened to and they need to know that their parents really listen to what they say. This is often easier said than done when junior is in the other room wailing, big brother and sister are brawling in the lounge room, the kettle is whistling and the television blaring. Nevertheless, the first five years of your child's life are the most important years for his communication development. His progress during this period may affect his future life. The quality of his communication skills will be partly dependent on his interaction with his parents, the most important people in his life.

In dealing with the information that follows it is important to remember that the age groups used are only approximate. For example, there is no need to panic if your one-year-old isn't saying too many single words, but if he reaches two and isn't using quite a number of single words then *don't wait* — seek professional help. Every individual is different, and nobody knows that more than a parent, but there is a range of normality that needs to be taken into account.

To make it easier for you to understand the development of normal language skills I have included samples of normal language within each age group. Most of these were collected from children that I have assessed over the years who had normal language skills for their age. The samples were collected by simply discussing school, home or favourite television programs, or by looking at books together. I made sure that I asked open-ended questions at all times to encourage a wide use of language structures. Toys were used to obtain language samples from the one- to three-year-olds.

You will notice I have written the samples as though the children had perfect articulation. (For a summary of what follows see Table 1, page 35.)

Hearing speech sounds

From the day your baby first emerges from his warm little cocoon he is exposed to a wide variety of sounds. He hears everything from car engines, to television soapies, to bathwater running and food processors whirring, and Mozart playing in the background. His first task is to separate these non-speech, environmental sounds from speech sounds.

Your baby's next step is to divide up the speech sounds into the individual sounds that form words. He must learn to tell the difference between sounds like /p/ and /b/, /t/ and /d/, so that he can differentiate between 'pin' and 'bin' and 'tin' and 'din'.

The child also learns to distinguish the sounds in his language from the sounds which aren't part of his language. Eventually he learns to retain the right sounds and disregard the wrong sounds.

Normal hearing is a prerequisite for developing these hearing skills, so do make sure that you have your baby's hearing checked by a specialist in the field — an audiologist — if you notice he is having the slightest difficulty responding to noise. Babies' hearing is often checked early in life by the clinic sister at your local baby health centre and then later on in life at school by the visiting nursing sister. However, if you have any worries at all it is best to seek the opinion of an audiologist. (See the Resources section at the back of the book for further details.)

Birth to three months

Babies learn the basic skills of communication from their very first cry. As your baby cries he is learning to make sounds in his voice box, he's feeling the air swishing around in his throat, nose and mouth, and he's learning how to change the pitch and the volume of his voice. He does all of this by moving from a whimper to that ear-piercing cry we are all too aware of. So the good news is that your bundle of joy is using all of his cries of hunger, pain, and pleasure to begin to communicate with you.

Three to four months

At about this age babies begin to 'coo', making isolated sounds other than cries, such as 'ah ah oo oo'. These are the vowel sounds and are made by vibrating the vocal cords without blocking the air flow. The basic vowels are /a, e, i, o, u/.

Other early developing sounds include consonants such as /k/

and /g/. These consonants are produced by the flow of air being interrupted by the articulators, which are the teeth, lips, tongue and the hard and soft palates.

Rewards like smiling, hugging and copying what your baby says will increase the amount of sounds that he makes, but they won't increase his range of sounds.

At this time babies also react to noises and to your voice by turning towards the source of the sound. Remember to be aware of this for your hearing check.

Four to six months

Before the baby utters his first word he is involved in a huge range of pre-verbal and non-verbal behaviours, all part of language development.

From about four months onwards your baby will regularly turn towards the sound of your voice. He will usually stop crying when you start to talk to him and he should recognise and respond to his own name. You may notice him using sounds other than crying to express anger. He may recognise words like 'mummy' and 'daddy' even when the words are used in conversational speech. He will listen to music, will make noises and babble a variety of sounds directly at you and others, and at times will stop when he hears the word 'no'. His repertoire of sounds may have expanded to include vowel sounds similar to /o/ and /u/.

Six to nine months

This is when your baby begins to 'babble', to experiment with a variety of sounds, some of which aren't in his native language.

Babbling at this age may be a string of connected sounds like 'gu gu', 'da da', 'ba ba'.

Most babies begin to babble using consonants at the back of the mouth such as /k/ and /g/, and vowels near the middle of the mouth such as /a/ as in 'bath'. The range of vowels babbled then extends to the front and back of the mouth and the consonants produced at the back of the mouth are often replaced by those made with the teeth, such as /t/ and /d/, and the lips such as /p/ and /b/. The pattern of babbling development is similar across different languages so, for example, French, English and Japanese babies all babble in the same way.

Between six and nine months of age babies also start using the intonation or sing-song patterns of adult speech. If intonation is not present it is an indication of possible hearing loss.

At this stage in their language development babies are involved in playing turn-taking games like 'peek-a-boo'. They also may sing along with familiar music. They will start to copy sounds and syllables used by you, if you do this for them directly, and will even start to use some gestures, such as shaking the head to mean 'no'. They may also recognise the names of some common objects, like 'bottle' and 'teddy'. They may understand some of your requests, for example, 'Look at dad' and 'Where's mum?'. If you show your child a colourful book at this age he will look at it for almost one minute before losing interest. Add to this his ability to stop whatever he's doing when his name is called, or in response to 'no', and you have a very skilful little individual.

Nine to twelve months

This is when your baby begins to 'jargon'. Jargoning is a long string of babbled syllables that sound very much like a foreign language. Occasionally you may recognise a real word in amongst the babbled syllables. A variety of sounds and intonation patterns continue to be used by your baby during this stage of development.

In addition to this, your baby now begins to copy sounds in his environment, such as cars and dogs.

Jargoning, although often uninterpretable by parents, is an exciting stage of speech development.

It is only at the end of these two phases of babbling and jargoning that different languages start to be distinguished. Prior to this your baby is capable of producing every sound of every language. Amazing, isn't it?

During this stage of development your baby will move from jargoning to becoming verbal, that is, to saying his first words, usually 'mama' and 'dada'. He will then move on to try to copy some of the words that you say, and by twelve months will probably be using about five real words consistently. He should be following simple commands like 'Don't touch' or 'Put that down', and will appear to understand an increasing number of words each week. He will now begin to look at your colourful picture book for approximately two minutes at a stretch.

Twelve to eighteen months

This is the all-important time when first words begin to appear. They may be the same syllable repeated over and over, such as 'mama' and 'dada' or single syllables such as 'do' for 'dog' and 'ba' for 'baby'.

Some children will continue their jargoning after their first words appear and may even continue using gestures to express what they mean for a short while.

Not only is this stage important for talking it's important for walking as well. Not long after the first words appear, the long-awaited moment finally arrives when your little one takes his first shaky steps. You may be surprised to find a previously vocal baby become very quiet once he starts walking. Don't be too worried as he's just concentrating on getting his walking under control. Once he's mastered this, he should return to his noisy self.

Around about this time children start to use intonation to signal differences between questions and their ever-present demands. The child's intonation pattern may not correspond to an adult intonation pattern, that is, something that sounds like a question may be meant as a demand.

The shift from jargoning to single words is a significant leap in speech development. Your child now has to make certain sounds in particular sequences, which requires planning and control. This is fairly difficult, so it is no wonder that at this time children may simplify their pronunciation of words by reducing lengthy words to smaller words. For example 'grandpa' may be 'papa' and 'grandma' may be 'mama'. Children will also tend to reduce single-syllable words to a very simple consonant-vowel combination. For example 'bottle' becomes 'bo' and 'drink' becomes 'di'. Among these shortened versions of words you occasionally will hear some of the lengthy real words clear as a bell.

Once the first 50 words or so are in use, your child's pattern of sound errors will become more noticeable. For example, he may use /t/ for /k/, so that 'car' becomes 'tar' and 'cat' becomes 'tat'. When it comes to blends — clusters of consonant sounds — such as /sl/ as in 'sleep' and /dr/ as in 'drum', you may find that your child just says one of the consonants, so that 'sleep' becomes 'seep' and 'drum' becomes 'dum'.

From the first single words to lengthy three-word sentences, your child works towards closing the gap between what he says and what he means to say.

From eighteen months of age onwards your child will have sufficiently developed his articulation skills for it to be apparent whether or not he is developing along normal lines. We have a list of sounds that the child should be able to use freely and accurately in his conversation at this stage in his development: /m, p, b, w, n, t, d/.

As mentioned earlier, learning to walk may interfere for a time with your child's language development. Don't panic, for he will resume his chattering once he has the difficult business of walking under control. At this stage he will perform an activity on request, for example he will follow an instruction of one or two directions such as 'Go get a nappy from the bedroom' or 'Pick up the ball and give it to daddy'.

He should now be using words rather than mainly gestures, and may even copy some two- and three-word sentences if encouraged. He will probably start to repeat some of the words that he hears you use in conversation as well as the sounds in his environment, such as cars and animals. He now recognises and will point to objects and pictures that you name for him and should recognise the names of many parts of the body. Memory skills develop and new words are associated and remembered by their categories, such as food, drink and clothing. If you place familiar objects in front of your child he should be able to identify two or more for you at this stage.

The first 50 words that your child develops are usually names of significant objects and people such as 'mummy', 'daddy', 'poo' and 'bath', common animal names such as 'pig' and 'duck'; and words that change the environment such as 'no' and 'more'. That is, they are either referential (referring to something), like 'duck', or expressive (expressing a social comment or a personal desire), like 'no'.

During this period a single word is often used to refer to many objects. For example anything with four legs may be 'dog', including a table. A single word may also be used to express several different meanings. For example the word 'drink' may mean 'I want a drink', 'The drink is gone', 'I want *that* drink' or 'Yuk, I don't want a drink'.

Language sample at twelve months

PLAYING WITH A DOLL'S HOUSE:
doll; up; boy; Matt [Matthew] chair; jump; more boy; that; look; wee; no; sock; shoe; nose; ear; bed.

As you can see, this language sample consists of mostly single words with a two-word combination. There is use of 'no' and 'more', a variety of nouns and some verbs, and a locative, the word 'up'.

Eighteen months to two years

Both competence and performance rapidly increase at this stage to the point where the child can select an item accurately from a choice of five objects; recognise and identify almost all common objects; begin to combine words into two-word combinations such as 'mum car' and 'daddy go'; refer to himself by his own name and even understand some complex sentences such as 'When we go to pick daddy up I'll buy you some lollies'. There are eight different word combinations that your child may use at this stage and they usually develop in the following order:

subject + object = daddy car (daddy sits in the car)

subject + action = daddy go

action + object = drive car

action + place = go car (daddy goes in the car)

possessor + possessed = daddy car

description + object or person = big car

demonstrator + object or person = that car

Your child may even use some three-word sentences such as 'Me go car'.

Language sample at eighteen months

PLAYING WITH DOLL'S HOUSE:
that doll; boy go; mum there; dolly up; more up; no more; that bed; big bed; sleep dolly; me sleep.

This language sample consists of two-word combinations. The child is using 'no' and 'more', a variety of verbs and nouns, the article 'that', locatives such as 'there' and 'up' and an adjective, 'big'.

Two to two-and-a-half years

From two years onwards your child's language skills develop at an ever-increasing rate. He will extend his skills to the point where he can demonstrate that he understands several action words by pointing out pictures that represent these actions. He will be able to recognise and point to pictures of family members such as mother, father, baby and grandmother. He will show an understanding of the functions of objects by answering questions such as 'What do you sleep in?' and 'What do you eat with?' He may even show an understanding of the adjectives 'big' and 'little' and should now recognise both the names and pictures of most common objects. Verbally, he should be using two- and three-word sentences frequently and should be able to repeat two or more numbers correctly and even name one colour. He will ask you for help in doing things now, such as going to the toilet.

Language sample at two years

PLAYING WITH A VARIETY OF TOYS:
look duck; oo that duck; sit down; more?; me jump; duck jump; quackquack; pig; look more pig mum; there more; pig jump; car; truck; that truck gone; no truck; dolly spoon; me spoon; oo more spoon; bottle mum?; bottle?

This language sample consists of mostly two-word combinations and some three-word combinations. A variety of nouns, verbs and locatives are used.

Two-and-a-half to five years

Between two-and-a-half to five years of age the child continues to develop the use of a varied range of rules for vocabulary, sentence meanings, and word and sentence structure. By five years of age your child has developed most of his language skills and should be functioning close to the adult model of language. For this reason children who have a language problem must have treatment before five years of age to achieve the best results.

Language sample at three years

LOOKING AT PICTURES OF A SKELETON AND A DOG IN A BOOK:
There's the stomach there. Me got one those.
I don't drink water. That make a stomach ache.
Me see inside. Open inside. Oo, you get yukky stuff out. That yukky stuff in there.
Me see dog mum. That big dog.
He's my dog. He's digging a hole.
He put that bone in.
He's going home now. His mum got more bones. His mum cook those bones. Where are more bones?

This language sample shows the increased length of each sentence as well as an increase in complexity. More questions are asked and more comments made about the state of things in general.

Language sample at four years

DESCRIBING A GAME OF 'FAMILIES' AT HOME:
He's been eating those. He was playing fathers. I was the baby and Mark was the dad. I watched the cooking things.
Mark fall over with Brett. Then Brett get up.
Mark was in the garage.
I was the mum. A pretend one. Then we were sitting on the blackboard. I hurt my knee. What was the slippery dip for? Why is that slippery dip not working? I get Mark to fix. Mark was the father. He can fix the slippery dip.

This sample shows a greater range of language and ideas. An

awareness of present and past tense is also evident, questions are asked, and there is use of the word 'and' to join sentences together.

Language sample at five years

DESCRIBING WHAT HAPPENS AT SCHOOL:
They have lots of books and toys. There's a dolly's house in the corner. I play with the dolly every single day. Then we go outside for lunch. We sit in the shed when it's raining. After lunch I play with my friends. Then we go back inside to do more work.
I do drawings for mum. She puts them on my cupboard cause she likes them. Then a boy rings a bell. Then mummy comes to get me and we go home then and eat something.

In this sample you can see the near-adult form of the language. Sentences are perfectly constructed and there is a sense of sequencing of time. Sentences are joined together by the use of 'and'.

TABLE 1

THE DEVELOPMENT OF COMMUNICATION SKILLS

Age	Communication Skills
birth–3 months	hearing develops learns to use voice box through crying
3–4 months	reacts to sound of voice cooing: vowels and some consonants e.g. /k/ and /g/
4–6 months	recognises and responds to own name makes noises at others recognises some words e.g. mummy, daddy, no develops vowel sounds similar to /o, e, u/
6–9 months	babbling intonation develops participates in turn-taking games sings along to music copies sounds and gestures recognises names of common objects
9–12 months	jargoning copies environmental sounds first words (about 5 of them) follows simple commands
12–18 months	develops intonation patterns for questions and demands more words but with simplified pronunciation sound errors will become noticeable performs activities on request copies 2- and 3-word sentences first 50 words of significant objects and people

Age	Communication Skills
18 months –2 years	2-word combinations and possible 3-word combinations understands complex sentences recognises and identifies all common objects
2–2½ years	understands action words points to picture to identify family members knows the functions of objects frequently uses 2- and 3-word sentences can repeat 2 or more numbers and name 1 colour can ask for help
2½–5 years	develops further rules for vocabulary, word and sentence structure by 5 years has developed most of language skills

KEY POINTS

- The first five years of your child's life are the most important years for both his articulation and language development.
- Although your child has an inborn capacity to develop speech, he must be provided with stimulation to develop normally.
- Have your child's hearing checked by an audiologist if you notice he has the slightest difficulty responding to noise.
- Young babies learn the basic skills of communication from their first cries.
- Before a child utters his first word he is involved in pre-verbal behaviours such as crying, babbling and jargoning; and non-verbal behaviours such as gesturing with the arms and face and pulling another person over to show them something.
- Don't worry if your child's use of single words is reduced as walking begins. This is usually only temporary.
- By five years of age a child has developed most of his language skills.

Chapter Three

HOW TO ASSESS YOUR CHILD'S COMMUNICATION SKILLS

Assessing your child's communication skills is not difficult, it just requires a bit of time and patience. You need to pay attention to his articulation, language skills, voice and fluency.

Articulation

There are two ways in which you can assess your child's articulation skills: one of these is in single words and the other is in conversation. In trying to decide which approach to adopt, keep in mind the child's ability to cooperate with you. Some children are 'outside angels' and will only cooperate with non-family members. If you know that your child *will* cooperate, then my advice is to use both approaches. Otherwise, I suggest that you find someone else you trust to work with your child.

If you wish to assess in single words then, using Table 2, the articulation word list provided on page 42, ask the child to say each word after you and note down any sounds that are incorrect. You will notice that the list covers most test sounds in every position in a word. For example, we test the sound /p/ at the front of a word ('pig'), in the middle of a word ('nappy'), and at the end of a word ('cup'). Your child may be able to say a sound in one position in a word but not in another. (It is only necessary to test the sounds appropriate for your child's age — see Table 3 on page 43. However, by testing all sounds you will have an overall picture of your child's skills. He may, for example, not be able to use some sounds appropriate for his age, but can use others which normally develop later.)

Having done this you will come up with a list of what are called 'error sounds'. By referring to Table 3 you can easily work out whether your child is saying all of the sounds that he should be for his age. This table is a compilation of various research studies into children's speech development, and does not differentiate between males and females. Most researchers agree that each age range should be looked at with a tolerance of plus or minus six months.

If you wish to assess your child's speech in conversation you can either tape him over a period of time then play back the tape and transcribe a list of error sounds, or you can try to write down the errors made as he is talking. Most parents find it easier to tape than write, as long as they can tape enough before the child becomes too aware of the tape recorder.

In my experience, give a child a tape recorder and a microphone and you have an instant stand-up comic routine complete with limericks, preschool songs and uncontrollable laughter. It is best, therefore, to tape the child while he is involved with something else, like playing and talking with a friend, or you could ask him questions while he is looking through a favourite book.

If you have a good ear for sounds then opt for writing the errors as you hear them, otherwise use the tape recorder. Remember you can always have a second and third go at each method if you need to.

Don't be surprised if you find that your child's error sounds are inconsistent. He might say /t/ for /k/ in 'cat' ('tat'), and he might say /d/ for /k/ in 'kite' ('dite'). This is not at all unusual and makes life far more interesting during the treatment procedure!

TABLE 2
ARTICULATION WORD LIST

h	hand		
ng		singing	song
p	pig	nappy	cup
m	me	hammer	drum
w	witch	flower	go
b	ball	baby	bib
n	nose	funny	run
d	doll	daddy	sad
t	toes	sitting	paint
k	car	looking	book
f	fish	laughing	cough
y	yes	buying	my
g	go	wagon	bag
l	light	lollie	ball
sh	shoe	fishing	fish
ch	chips	butcher	watch
j	jump	budgie	fridge
s	sun	messy	bus
z	zoo	lizard	eyes
r	rabbit	sparrow	
v	vegetable	oven	glove
th	thank you	Matthew	bath
th	this	mother	bathe

TABLE 3
THE DEVELOPMENT OF CONSONANTS

$1\frac{1}{2}$–2 years	m p b w n t d
2–$2\frac{1}{2}$ years	m p b w n t d h (ng k g)
$2\frac{1}{2}$–$3\frac{1}{2}$ years	m p b w n t d h ng k g f y s (l)
$3\frac{1}{2}$–$4\frac{1}{2}$ years	m p b w n t d h ng k g f v y s z l (r) ch j
$4\frac{1}{2}$–+ years	m p b w n t d h ng k g f v y s z l r ch j sh zh (as in 'measure') th (as in 'thin') th (as in 'this')

PAMELA GRUNWELL, *CLINICAL PHONOLOGY*, SECOND EDITION, CROOM HELM LTD, KENT, 1987.
(USED BY PERMISSION)

Language

When assessing your child's language skills you need to rely very much on listening to him in conversation. Does he sound like other children of his age? Does he seem to leave out a lot of little words in a sentence? Is his sentence construction poor and are his words always back-to-front?

Without the help of a speech pathologist it is difficult to gain an accurate assessment of language. However, observing other children of a similar age and maturity can provide the parent with an informal judgement of any problem areas. The same is true for comprehension skills. Most parents know when their child cannot understand what is being said — one tell-tale sign is having to continually repeat what you say to your child. Remember it may not be hearing that is the problem but comprehension. Refer back to the information on normal language development (Chapter 2) and you will be able to establish your child's level of language. Is he doing most of the things he should be doing at his age?

Fluency

Stuttering is a very common problem and is something that parents are easily alerted to because of the distress that it causes both the child and themselves. It is best to listen for any significant hesitancy, any repetition of syllables, words or phrases. Also look for any evidence of frustration in the child. He may well express this readily by saying: 'I can't say that'. A sensible parent can make a very good judgement of their child's fluency. This topic will also be dealt with in more detail in Chapter 4.

Voice

Assessing a child's voice can be easy as long as you remain unbiased. We become so used to the sound of our family members' voices that we tend to take them very much for granted. In a child, problems are indicated by hoarseness or harshness in the voice, use of too low or too high a pitch, any complete loss of voice, or a constant sore throat. We will be dealing with voice problems in more detail in Chapter 5.

Assessing your child's communication skills yourself takes time and patience, but it is well worth the effort. Professional assistance should be sought as soon as possible, of course, but in the meantime you don't have to feel helpless or in the dark.

KEY POINTS

- You can assess your child's articulation skills by checking single words, taping whole conversations or recording the errors on paper as you hear them.
- It is not unusual for a child's articulation errors to be inconsistent.
- To assess language skills you must rely on listening to a child's conversation. You will, however, only end up with an informal judgement. Proper language assessment can only be made by a speech pathologist.
- You should check the quality of your child's voice and his fluency.

Chapter Four

STUTTERING

Of all the communication disorders occurring in children, stuttering is the most disconcerting. It is a problem that appears virtually overnight and is often characterised by its appearance and disappearance at regular or irregular intervals.

Stuttering affects every aspect of an individual's life, and is the source of much frustration. It makes a person feel helpless and out of control. There are a great many 'old wives' tales' that relate to stuttering, and they too can cause distress.

Stuttering usually appears between the ages of two and seven. If it appears much later than this it may be quite severe from the outset.

In the two- to seven-year-old age bracket stuttering normally develops in a pattern, moving from repetition of syllables ('mu mu mu mummy') and words ('mummy mummy mummy'), to repetition of phrases ('I want I want mummy') or stretching out a sound in a word ('mmmmmmmummy').

If the stuttering continues to develop, 'blocking', the inability to say the word at all, may occur. It is often characterised by a degree of tension in the voice and/or on the face when the child tries to initiate a word but can't. Blocking can be frightening for both the child and the parent.

A range of secondary behaviours may exist when the child has a stuttering moment. These range from blinking and rolling the eyes back in the head, to movement of the head, hands, arms or feet. Some children with a severe problem may show a great deal of tension in the face and a posturing of the lip or other facial muscles. Children who are severe stutterers may also avoid certain words in their conversation and substitute others in their place.

There are some characteristics that are common to most people who stutter. It appears that a person who may stutter in conversation may not necessarily stutter if he sings, whispers, reads or talks in unison with another person. Similarly there are times when a person is more likely stutter, for example, when they are excited, overtired or upset and emotional.

The current philosophy is that stuttering is caused by a combination of genetic and environmental factors. Because each individual can stutter under such different circumstances it has proved a difficult area of investigation for researchers. Stuttering does, however, occur in more males than females, the ratio being three to one.

It is true that emotional factors are connected with stuttering, but it is important for doctors and parents to understand that stuttering is not in itself an emotional problem. Rather, it seems that the stuttering behaviour itself may cause emotional problems.

Assessing and Treating Stuttering

Contrary to the popular belief that stuttering should be ignored, it is wise to seek professional guidance as soon as the problem emerges.

Between the ages of two and five all children go through a period of development in their language where they repeat words over and over. This is called 'normal dysfluency'. If you listen to an average three-year-old you will probably hear this happening and notice that the child is not even aware of it.

Because of this stage of normal dysfluency, if you are concerned, it is important that your child be assessed to determine if he is going through this stage or is in fact stuttering. A speech pathologist will determine this by assessing the types of dysfluencies, for example are they simple repetitions of words or is there a certain amount of blocking. The number of stuttered words or syllables is calculated and any secondary characteristics are noted, along with the child's degree of awareness of the problem.

If a child exhibits a good deal of blocking and prolongs sounds, as well as blinking the eyes and becoming frustrated, it is very likely that he is stuttering. If he is using a number of easy repetitions of words, no tension or secondary characteristics are evident, and he is seemingly unaware of any problem, then it is likely that he is going through a stage of normal dysfluency.

The treatment of stuttering in both children and adults has improved tremendously recently. If a child receives treatment immediately then the prognosis for removing the stutter is very good. If the stutter emerges when the child is eleven or older, it may take more complicated treatment to resolve the problem, but the results are still generally very good.

If your child is young, a good way to deal with the problem is to encourage him to talk slowly all the time. Demonstrate the difference between fast and slow by using toy cars and your own fast and slow talking. Slowing down in itself should have a positive effect upon the stuttering behaviour. Continue to do this all the time, encouraging other family members to do the same.

In addition to this, set aside ten to twenty minutes at least once a day for playing and talking with your child on his own. You can play with toys or look through picture books. Every time you hear him stutter say to him: 'That was bumpy talking, try saying that again slowly'. If your child repeats the phrase or sentence fluently then reward him immediately with hugs or some other reward and make sure you say: 'That was good talking, I didn't hear any bumpy talking'. If he can't make the repetition fluently then give him one more try before saying 'good try' and moving on with the conversation. Make sure you vary the games, and make sure that you give the child plenty of rewards for good, slow talking.

The sad fact about stuttering is that even after the problem has been remediated and the child is totally stutter free, it is possible that the stutter may re-emerge later in life. In such instances a booster program of treatment is usually all that is required, but in some cases, it will continue to re-emerge throughout life.

If your child's stuttering is severe it is wise to try to encourage slow talking, but do nothing more before seeking professional intervention.

It is important to try to ascertain whether your child is being teased by anybody and to eliminate this if at all possible. Try to eliminate any negative reactions to the stuttering.

No matter how old the child is it is a good idea to discuss your management of the stuttering with caregivers, teachers, friends and relatives so that the child receives consistent feedback.

Children who stutter need all the support they can get. Fortunately, there are many successful programs available, both intensive and non-intensive, as well as self-help support groups.

KEY POINTS

- Stuttering usually appears between the ages of two and seven.
- If your child develops a stutter you should seek professional advice immediately.
- All children go through a stage of normal dysfluency — repeating words — between the ages of two and five.
- If the child is young, encourage him to talk slowly all the time.
- Discuss your approach to the stuttering with caregivers, teachers, friends and relatives so that the child receives consistent feedback.

CHAPTER FIVE

VOICE DISORDERS

Vocal abuse

Children who persistently shout or scream are overusing and abusing their voices. This is called vocal abuse.

The child who screams in the playground or at football training each week, the child who imitates Rambo or the child who pretends that his bike is a motorbike and makes the appropriate noises is in danger of developing a voice disorder. Even constantly and noisily clearing the throat can eventually damage the voice. Living in a noisy environment will obviously exacerbate the problem, and dust in the air can also be harmful.

Shouting and screaming can cause little lumps called 'nodules' to develop on the vocal cords. Usually the nodules can be reduced by speech pathology intervention but if they are well advanced surgery will be necessary. When nodules exist it seems that only one episode of vocal abuse during a whole week is enough for the problem to persist.

Treating vocal abuse

Treatment of vocal abuse usually focuses on identifying and eliminating the situation in which abuse occurs. If this is impossible, the aim is to reduce the abusive behaviour, for example, getting the child to reduce the number of screams or shouts in the playground.

For some children the threat of possible surgery is a strong motivating force, but for others, a stringent reward/punishment system is necessary. For example, if Tom screams and shouts every lunchtime at school we need to set up a reinforcement program where his teacher or best friend records the number of times he shouts or screams during the lunch break. Often, if the child is older, he can record his own vocal abuse or avoidance of it. We promise Tom that when he gets his shouts and screams under control, that is, non-existent, he can have a family outing to anywhere he chooses. Furthermore, for every day that he continues to shout and scream at school he loses television viewing time. This may seem tough, but in some cases strategies such as this are the only way in which surgery can be avoided.

Puberphonia

An unusual voice disorder can occur in teenage males, when, after the voice has 'broken' around the time of puberty, they cling to their higher pitched or 'old' voice and use this consistently. It is called puberphonia. The voice is abnormally high and they are often ridiculed by others for sounding like a girl. The change in personality that occurs when, through treatment, these young men acquire their 'proper' voice is often astounding. They can change from highly strung and intensely shy individuals who refuse to talk at school to very confident young men.

If the patient is very resistant to change, as is sometimes the case, the speech pathologist may refer him to a psychologist or psychiatrist for treatment concurrent with, or prior to, speech pathology intervention.

Vocal Misuse

Excessive contraction of the muscles used for breathing, vocalising sounds or resonating is called vocal misuse. It can result in a voice which is excessively high, low, breathy, harsh, loud or soft. Although this doesn't produce as dramatic a change in the vocal cords as nodules, it can cause swelling and irritation of the vocal cords. This results in poor or inappropriate vocal quality for a child's age or sex.

Unlike vocal abuse, vocal misuse is not easily treated at home. Professional help from a speech pathologist is necessary. Children respond well to the treatment for misuse and quite easily develop new patterns that place far less effort upon the muscles used in voice production.

Resonance Disorders

When a child speaks in a way that interferes with the normal resonance, or tone, of his voice he has a resonance disorder. Habitual placement of the tongue too far forward in the mouth, for example, can result in a 'thin' sounding voice.

Habitual placement of the tongue too far back in the mouth results in what is called 'cul-de-sac' resonance — the voice isn't projected and a muffled, hollow tone is produced.

When the cavities of the nose or mouth aren't closed off from each other on sounds which require a build-up of air in the mouth such as /p, f, sh/, the air is directed up into the nose and can even be forced out through the nose in what is almost a snort. This is called hypernasality and is common in children with a cleft palate. It may also be the result of a functional problem, where the child has not learnt to close off the nasal or oral cavities when necessary.

The opposite of hypernasality is hyponasality when there is too little nasal resonance and the child sounds as though he has a cold.

All resonance disorders should be assessed and treated by a speech pathologist.

Because voice disorders can be serious, it is essential that both a speech pathologist and an ear, nose and throat specialist are consulted. The speech pathologist will assess the voice, and treat the problem if necessary, and the ear, nose and throat specialist will determine whether there is any structural problem with the vocal cords.

KEY POINTS

- Vocal abuse is a disorder where someone persistently abuses their voice, risking damage to their vocal cords.
- Treatment of vocal abuse focuses on identifying and eliminating, as much as possible, the situations where vocal abuse occurs. If the nodules on the vocal cords caused by the abuse are advanced, then surgery will be necessary.
- If a male whose voice has broken clings to his old higher pitched voice, professional treatment should be sought.
- Vocal misuse occurs when someone uses excessive contraction of the muscles used in voice production.
- Poor resonance affects the tone of the voice and can be caused by the tongue being placed too far forward, too far back in the mouth or the inability to close off the oral or nasal cavity when necessary.
- Professional treatment by a speech pathologist is required for problems of vocal misuse and resonance.

58

Chapter Six

ARTICULATION DISORDERS

Articulation disorders form a large part of any speech pathologist's caseload. Poor articulation is usually the first problem identified by parents, teachers or health care professionals. To accurately understand articulation we need to firstly understand the processes that result in the articulation of a sound.

The speech mechanism

The production of speech consists of four phases: respiration, phonation, resonation and articulation.

Respiration in its simplest form involves the exchange of gases between us and our environment — breathing in and out. For the production of speech, however, it is more than this. The air that is expelled from the body on breathing out actually serves to power the sound-producing mechanism — the vocal cords. Air also is used to make the speech signal louder once it has been produced. Children who have significant difficulties in breathing may have problems with their voice. It may fade off because they run out of air, or may simply be too soft for others to hear. Because air is used to produce many of the sounds in our language, for example /p, t, k, sh, s, h/, a child may have difficulty in producing these sounds accurately if his respiration is poor.

Phonation is the production of sound. This is performed by passing a stream of air through the larynx or voice box and the vocal cords. The vocal cords are long, smooth, rounded bands of muscle which are positioned in the larynx and they lengthen and shorten, tense and relax, and open and close. During normal breathing the vocal cords are spaced fairly widely apart and the air stream is free to move past the cords without being blocked.

When the air stream is set into vibration to make a sound the vocal cords are blown apart then simply snap back into position again, ready to be blown apart again by the next build-up of air pressure. In the normal production of a vowel sound, such as /a/, this occurs at a rate of about 133 vibrations per second for men and about 235 vibrations per second for women. It is even higher for children. Damage to the vocal cords can result in them not vibrating as they should, and the voice produced may be breathy or harsh in quality.

Resonation is the amplification of a particular sound. This is performed by the mouth, nose, hard and soft palates, pharynx and even the sinuses. These structures work to give each sound its particular tone. If the nasal area isn't closed off correctly from the oral areas during the production of sounds requiring air flow then the sounds may be distorted and difficult for the listener to understand. When the sinuses are blocked there is a lack of resonance and we tend to sound like we do when we have a cold.

Articulation is the ability to produce the sounds of language. It is the most important aspect of the speech mechanism. Articulation involves the use of the articulators: the lips, cheeks, teeth, tongue, and the soft and hard palates and the pharynx (used with the tongue). We manipulate these structures and muscles in various ways to make the sounds language requires. This task may appear to most of us to be a very ordinary one, but it is in fact a very delicate procedure involving fine coordination of nerves and muscles. Babies are born with the ability to articulate all the sounds of all languages.

What causes articulation disorders?

The development of normal articulation skills depends upon a number of factors. First, we know that there needs to be an innate or prebirth ability to form good sounds. Little is known for certain regarding this area despite the number of theories that exist on the topic.

Secondly, we need to have normal hearing. If the child is not hearing a sound correctly it is difficult for him to reproduce it accurately. Hearing problems in children under five years of age can often be caused by ear infections. If such an infection is severe the ear-drum may burst, and scar tissue that forms as a result may impede the normal movement of the ear-drum. Children who have numerous ear infections are therefore at risk of hearing loss and, consequently, abnormal speech development.

Thirdly, the development of normal articulation depends upon the structure and function of all of the articulators being normal. In some cases there may be damage to the nerves of the muscles of the lips, tongue or palates, restricting their movement.

Children who have cerebral palsy usually experience articulation difficulties and may also have problems with respiration, phonation and resonance. Children who have Down's syndrome who are born with abnormally large tongues, may also have articulation problems. Some children may have dental abnormalities that are sufficiently severe to affect speech development, for example a child with a cleft palate may develop misplaced teeth, turned teeth or even grow extra teeth.

It is possible that some children can be predisposed to an articulation disorder because there is a significant history of a speech problem in the family. Little is known about genetic predisposition to particular speech disorders, but genetics apart, if one or more family members have a speech problem, they will be providing the child with an incorrect model of how a sound is produced.

Errors of articulation generally fall into three categories. The child will either substitute another sound for the correct sound, that is, he will say /th/ for /s/ as in the case of a lisp; he will omit the sound altogether from his words, for example, leaving out the /h/ from 'house' which becomes 'ouse'; or he will distort the sound and turn it into a combination of two sounds, for example 'red' becomes 'wred', or a sound foreign to his language.

Children with mild articulation problems will only have difficulties with substitutions and omissions, but unfortunately those whose problems are more severe often display a combination of at least two types of error.

See Chapter 3 for information about how to assess your child's articulation ability.

Tongue-tie

Being 'tongue-tied' can be a real problem for some children. A 'tongue-tie' is a rare condition where the small section of skin connecting the tip of the tongue to the floor of the mouth is very short. This can limit the child's ability to move the tongue up, down, in, out and from side to side. To tell if your child has a tongue-tie you can ask him to move his tongue from side to side, ask him to try and touch his upper lip with the tip of his tongue and try and touch his chin with the tip of his tongue. Observe any problems the child may have in carrying out these movements. A child with a tongue-tie will have restricted movement of the tongue when trying to lift, lower or move it from side to side. Another way to tell is to ask your child to stick out his tongue. The normal tongue has a rounded curve to it but if it has a tongue-tie it will look as though it is almost divided into two separate sections. There will be a little area at the tip where the muscle is almost pulled back into the tongue, giving it a shape similar to the letter 'w' rather than the letter 'u'.

A tongue-tie can sometimes be noted and corrected at birth by surgery, or at a later date by clipping the tissue connecting the floor of the mouth to the tongue. Many children who have a mild tongue-tie don't have any problems moving their tongue or in the development of speech sounds. Children with a severe tongue-tie have great difficulty, especially in the development of sounds that require the tongue to be lifted up to the roof of the mouth, for example, the sounds /t, l, d, n/. These children may benefit from surgery, however surgery alone may not necessarily correct the articulation disorder. Speech therapy may still be needed.

Lisping

I often get asked about lisping. Although lisping can appear cute when the child is young, it can be of great concern and embarrassment to a teenager and a professional handicap to those wishing to pursue a job that requires good articulation skills. Actors, radio announcers, journalists and barristers often spend a great deal of time and money having a lisp 'left over from childhood' fixed by a speech pathologist.

Lisps can develop for a variety of reasons. The child may develop incorrect placement of the tongue during the time when his two front teeth are missing. If this period is extended for one reason or another then the abnormal pattern may become a habit and the child will be left with a lisp even when his front teeth have grown.

A lisp may also develop by habitually placing the tongue too far forward in the mouth. If the tongue is forward at all times, it is in a ready position to jump out past the teeth on the production of the /s/ and /z/ sounds. If a child has an open bite, where there is a large gap between the top and bottom rows of teeth, it is even easier for the tongue to protrude forward during speech.

Treating articulation disorders

The degree of severity of articulation problems varies greatly. Some children can say a sound clearly in single sentences but do not use it correctly in conversational speech. Other children have difficulty saying a sound in a phrase or a single word. Still others may have problems producing the sound on its own no matter how many times someone demonstrates it for them.

All these children need individual work on each problem sound in a structured way so that they will eventually be able to produce the sound accurately in conversation all the time.

A speech pathologist will start by teaching the child the correct positioning of the articulators for the problem sound and indicate how the sound should sound when produced correctly. She will then move on to train him to say the new correct sound pattern in a series of nonsense words. When the child can produce the sound correctly in these contexts then the task is made more difficult by working on it in real words. The child is first asked to say each word after the speech pathologist so that she can provide him with a good model to copy. Mirrors are often used to help the child observe the correct positioning of the articulators and on each attempt the child is given very specific feedback — whether the sound was correct and why, or whether the sound was incorrect, and what to do to fix it.

Once the child can produce the words accurately after the speech pathologist has said them he is asked to say the words all on his own as the therapist points to pictures of the words. The next step is to say the sound in a word in a phrase after the therapist, and then on his own. Once the child has accomplished the phrases, the therapist moves on to using the sound in simple sentences. Again the child repeats the sentences after the therapist and then on his own. At every point along the way feedback is given both to improve performance and to encourage a positive attitude to the work. The therapist will make sure that the work is made fun and interesting.

After the child has achieved success with sentences, the next step is to practise the sound by filling in the missing words in a story that the therapist composes. The story can be as silly and amusing as the child desires. Once the child becomes used to the story he is asked to say the story on his own and even make up his own silly story using pictures.

Achieving the new correct sound with accuracy in everyday conversation often takes a great deal of effort from all sides. Because the child spends far more time with the parents than the speech pathologist, much of the responsibility for reminding the child to use the correct sound rests with the parents. The speech pathologist will have numerous helpful hints and ideas that parents can use to work on the sound at home.

Some children with articulation problems are in treatment for as little as four to six weeks, while others are in treatment for two or three years. The length of treatment obviously depends on the severity of the problem, how quickly the child progresses in treatment, and how much follow-up work can be done in between treatment sessions at home or at school. Although most teachers have a heavy load of commitments, they can often find the time to help with a speech therapy program if it is provided and well explained by the speech pathologist.

The attitudes of both the parents and the child to the problem and the work to be done are obviously a crucial factor in the treatment process. Parents who perceive an articulation problem with the gravity that it deserves are far more motivated to work with their child at home. On the other hand, an over-zealous or strict parent can hamper progress by placing too much pressure upon the child to move through treatment at a rapid pace. If your child is receiving treatment you should aim to strike a balance between lots of encouragement, positive feedback and constructive criticism, to promote a healthy attitude all round.

The child with a relatively mild articulation difficulty, and who has normal intelligence, well-motivated parents, works hard in all treatment sessions and who has no other contributing communication difficulties, will move through treatment fairly rapidly. The child who has a severe problem, belatedly diagnosed, who has other contributing problems such as a hearing loss or intellectual handicap, and whose parents fail to do any follow-up work at home, is likely to move slowly through treatment, despite the speech pathologist's best efforts.

KEY POINTS

- The development of normal articulation skills depends on the innate ability to form good sounds, normal hearing skills and the normal structure and function of all the articulators.
- There are three kinds of articulation errors: substituting, omitting and distorting the sounds.
- Treating articulation disorders involves working on individual sounds in a structured hierarchy of contexts.

You should be a little more attentive, try to concentrate on our instructions or you won't comprehend
uhh?

Chapter Seven

PROBLEMS WITH LANGUAGE COMPREHENSION

For many children the meaning of much of their own language is a mystery. They cannot understand what others are saying to them and receive what can only be described as a message similar to a garbled telegram. For those who have a severe handicap in understanding language they may only comprehend the few simple words that are significant and have meaning for them, for example, if asked to: 'Pick up the ball and give it to daddy', the child may only understand the words 'ball' and 'daddy'.

For the parent who feels that their child is understanding everything, to be told that he has a comprehension problem often appears ludicrous, and they may take a great deal of convincing. It is no wonder that many parents feel this way. Even teachers can be disbelieving. After all didn't their child go into the next room and get a nappy when his mother requested him to do so? Didn't he put the piece of rubbish in the bin when his father told him to? Didn't he come and sit on the mat at the front of the classroom just as the teacher requested?

As parents, we often don't realise the extent to which a child with a comprehension problem relies upon habit, observation of others and other contextual clues and on the amount of gesturing we do when we request that something be done. When the child goes into the baby's room to get a nappy for his mother he may be responding to a number of clues in his environment — the baby is on the change table being changed and this is something that occurs numerous times throughout the day. The child knows by habit what is required of him in this situation and even if he comprehends only the word 'nappy' in his mother's request he will be able to respond accurately. When his father asks the child to put the rubbish in the bin he may be pointing at the bin and may even hand the rubbish to the child. Again, the child may respond to the word 'bin' alone and still be able to carry out the request accurately. Furthermore, if the teacher asks all the children to come and sit on the mat at the front of the classroom and every other child does this, it is no wonder that the child with the comprehension problem follows suit and thus appears to be understanding everything that is said to him.

Many parents become distressed when they are told that their child has a comprehension problem, assuming that comprehension is related to intelligence. They worry that their child may be intellectually handicapped in some way. It is true that children who are intellectually handicapped usually have language comprehension difficulties, but this does not mean that all children who have comprehension difficulties are intellectually handicapped.

How do you know if your child has a problem?

So how do you know if your child has a comprehension problem? The first thing to do is to become aware of how often you use gestures when asking your child to do something. Try to stop yourself gesturing and see if your child can still perform the task. The next step is to remove as many contextual clues as possible. You can do this by asking him to do something that is out of the ordinary in some way. For example, if you always ask your child to get a nappy from the bedroom, move the nappies somewhere else before you ask your child to fetch one.

Some parents first become concerned when they find that their child is not progressing well at school despite the fact that he tries extremely hard. If your child constantly looks blank when you are giving him an instruction, then the chances are that he has a comprehension problem. If he consistently misinterprets what is said to him, puts on his running shoes when he was asked to put on his school shoes, or puts paper in the garbage bin when he was asked to put it on the table, then he may also have a comprehension problem.

There are many different kinds of comprehension problems. Some children may show a lack of understanding of particular categories of words, for example, nouns or verbs or adjectives. Others may show a lack of understanding of other parts of grammar, say personal pronouns such as 'he' and 'she', getting them confused or leaving them out of their language altogether. Many children have difficulties understanding verb tenses and the concept of time, that is, present, past, and future. Other children may understand individual meanings of words but have difficulty when the words are placed in relationship to one another in a sentence. All of these problems can be treated by a speech pathologist.

Language comprehension difficulties may be caused by one or more of a variety of other problems. Children who have a hearing impairment, for example, almost always show some deficit in their language comprehension. Children with learning difficulties may also have significant problems in the area of language comprehension. But for many children who have normal intelligence and no other obvious contributing factors, the cause of their comprehension difficulties remains unknown. For some reason the child's innate ability to comprehend language is impaired and he simply doesn't develop the concepts appropriate for his age, as expected. Sometimes the child's innate ability was good but his development of comprehension skills ceased at a certain point. On rare occasions it has been found that a child's comprehension deficit can be directly related to a lack of stimulation from the parents. Orphans who spend their early years in institutions where stimulation of all kinds may be limited are no doubt candidates for language comprehension problems.

As already mentioned, children who are intellectually handicapped often have major problems in the area of language comprehension. Autistic children may also have similar problems. A speech pathologist often has to teach these children the meaning of simple words such as 'cup', 'spoon', 'dog', or 'walk'.

Treating comprehension problems

Children with comprehension difficulties are taught the meaning of words by being exposed to specific pictures and objects. If it is an object, then the function of the object is demonstrated. The child is guided in using the object correctly in many different contexts until he demonstrates an understanding of the word. If the word is an action word, such as 'walk', then the action is demonstrated by the therapist and the child is encouraged to perform the action himself. Pictures are presented that represent other people performing this action. It is again shown in a variety of contexts until the child demonstrates an understanding of the meaning of the word. Although a child with a severe problem moves slowly through therapy, he can eventually be taught all the language concepts appropriate for his age.

If you are concerned about your child's comprehension skills, do seek professional advice. Speech pathologists have the necessary test equipment and knowledge of what is normal at each age range to be able to determine the state of your child's comprehension skills. The comprehension tests used by speech pathologists provide structured situations where the comprehension of specific items can be tested one by one, without the interference of routine or gestures. Also, because speech pathologists are so used to dealing with children with comprehension difficulties, the tell-tale signs and symptoms of such a problem are glaringly obvious to them.

Many parents are actually relieved to find out that their child has a real problem and is not just being naughty and not carrying out instructions. It can be very frustrating for parents to have their child constantly misinterpreting what they say to him. Parents can assist their child by talking in shorter sentences and by talking more slowly than usual. The child should be encouraged to always ask the parents to repeat what they have said if he has not understood. Repeating a sentence may be all that is needed for the child to understand. If the problem is severe, gestures may be used to help.

Similarly, children of school age should always be encouraged to ask the teacher directly when they don't understand something that has been said. It is important to note that children with comprehension difficulties are often labelled disruptive in the classroom as they may be constantly asking the child next to them what they are supposed to be doing.

If a comprehension problem exists in conjunction with other areas of difficulty, like articulation (Chapter 6) or expressive language difficulties (Chapter 8), then the process of treatment is slower. Everything has to be explained simply, slowly and numerous times. Even the most simple instructions can produce a blank look the first few times they are given. Many things have to be physically demonstrated to make sure that the child understands exactly what is required. All of this takes up treatment time but is absolutely essential for the acquisition of improved communication skills.

KEY POINTS

- Comprehension problems cause children to have difficulty understanding what others are trying to say.
- It is often difficult to know if your child has a comprehension problem because they can often understand a good deal from the context of a given situation.
- Having a comprehension problem does not mean that a child is intellectually handicapped.
- Comprehension problems should be professionally assessed and treated by a speech pathologist.

Chapter Eight

EXPRESSIVE LANGUAGE DISORDERS

We all use language to have our needs met, to express how we feel, to instruct others and to generally change the environment around us. When we talk to someone who shares our language we assume that they use it in the same way that we do, inasmuch as the words we use and how we put them together have the same meaning for each of us. If we don't have this similarity in language it is very difficult for us to communicate.

For the child who has a severe expressive language disorder, communicating the most basic needs can seem like climbing Mount Everest. First he has to think of the right words to use, then he has to get them into the correct order in his head, then get them from his brain to the point of articulation. A complicated process indeed, but one that those of us with normal expressive language skills take for granted.

Many children with expressive language difficulties withdraw inside themselves, often to the point where they refuse to join in activities, never ask questions in class or in the playground, and in some cases simply stop talking altogether.

How do you recognise an expressive language disorder?

Many parents are not aware that their child has an expressive language delay. They assume that he is just using 'baby talk' and that he will grow out of it. The fact that it is normal at certain ages to leave out certain parts of grammar, or say 'me' instead of

'I' as language is developing, further confuses the issue for parents. When they compare their child with other children they come to the conclusion that it's nothing to be concerned about. The 'he'll grow out of it' syndrome is a common phenomenon, also unfortunately subscribed to by many general practitioners who know very little about language development. The advice to wait until he starts school, as I have said before, is disastrous.

If you are concerned that your child leaves words out of sentences (often the little ones) or mixes up the order of words, then it is best to have him assessed by a speech pathologist. It is also important to note that although starting school often gives children confidence and a stimulating verbal environment, it alone is not enough to correct the complex problem of an expressive language difficulty.

The causes of expressive language problems

Expressive language difficulties, like other communication difficulties, can occur for a variety of reasons. In some cases there is a history of retarded language development, or a history of communication problems requiring treatment within the family. It is not uncommon for a speech pathologist to end up treating a number of children in the one family. Sometimes the disorders will be similar in nature, at other times they will be diverse, for example, one child with a language problem and another with a stuttering problem.

Hearing impairment is another factor which can cause expressive language disorders. If the child does not hear the language structures being used, he may never understand the meanings of words. If he does not understand a word, he can't use it. Similarly, if a child does not hear the ways in which sentences are constructed he may construct his own sentences 'back to front'.

Children who are intellectually handicapped or who have severe emotional disorders such as autism fail to develop expressive language in a normal way. Children who have suffered head injury usually also have expressive language difficulties. Children with a learning difficulty almost always have significant expressive language difficulties. Occasionally children who were hospitalised for long periods of time or severely deprived of any stimulation early on in life present with an expressive language delay.

With a large percentage of young children who have expressive language delay, the cause is unknown. It appears that they are either delayed in their development of language from the start, i.e. from the moment they first use words, or they develop normally to a certain age and then for some reason development ceases. It can sometimes be more difficult for parents to accept that a problem exists if the cause is unknown.

Parents are often deeply concerned that they, in some way, may have caused the language delay. They feel responsible for not stimulating their child enough or for neglecting him because of the arrival of another baby. I very seldom see a family where the child's language delay can be directly related to lack of stimulation, but this does not mean that early stimulation is not vital to normal development.

Treating the problem

As part of a speech pathology assessment the therapist will often take what is called a spontaneous language sample by recording the child's speech in everyday conversation. By looking at a large sample the therapist can analyse it for the language skills necessary for the relevant age range. I often ask parents to record their child at home so that I can compare language use in the clinic with that used in the home environment. This information, coupled with the results of more formal language testing, will provide the therapist with a clear idea of how a child is functioning. Is his expressive language age the same as his chronological age? Is he constructing sentences that are appropriately complex for his age? Is he using all the parts of grammar that he should? The child's assessment will have provided her with a list of grammatical structures that need to be worked on.

If the child has a problem with the meanings of words, the first task will be to work on one word until the child fully comprehends the meaning of that word. Once the speech pathologist is convinced of this, she will work the child through a series of steps to encourage verbal use of the word in a large number of contexts. When the child is using the word appropriately 80 per cent of the time in his sentences all on his own, then the therapist and the parents will begin the task of encouraging carryover of this new word into the child's everyday conversation. This carryover procedure can take a great deal of time, patience and hard work, but the results will be well worth the effort. The confidence that the child will gain from merely sounding like other children his own age will be a reward in itself.

Sentence construction skills can be worked on by providing both auditory and visual models of how the sentence should sound and what it looks like when the words are in the correct order. The child is systematically taught various forms of sentence construction. For example: subject-verb-locative — 'John is walking home'; or subject-verb-adjective — 'John is happy'.

For those children who aren't of reading age or who have extremely poor reading skills, coloured blocks, or other colour-coded materials, can be used to show the child a correct sentence order. The child may be shown that we put a red block on the table first to represent the subject, then a blue block for the verb and a green block for the locative.

Parents can assist in the remediation of an expressive language disorder by constantly using the part of grammar or particular sentence construction being worked on by the pathologist. This provides the child with numerous examples of the targeted language item in everyday conversation. Reminding the child of the correct form every time he makes a mistake and praising him every time he gets it right will help him with the carryover of the new skill into normal conversation.

KEY POINTS

- A child with an expressive language handicap has difficulty finding and using the right words in the right order to express what he means.
- Some of the most obvious signs of an expressive language problem are leaving out parts of the grammar and getting the words in the wrong order.
- A speech pathologist will start treatment after an extensive analysis of your child's everyday conversation.

Chapter Nine

LEARNING DIFFICULTIES

There has been an increase in the level of awareness of learning difficulties in recent times. More children are being diagnosed as having a problem and more parents are realising that they themselves had similar problems at school. Despite all of this, however, there is still much ignorance about the nature and treatment of learning difficulties. For example, the speech pathologist is usually the last person on a long list of professionals to whom learning-disabled children are referred. People assume that a child should only be referred to a speech pathologist if something is wrong with his speech. In fact a speech pathologist can offer a great deal of advice on other related matters.

Children with learning difficulties display a broad spectrum of symptoms ranging from fine and gross motor disturbances to visual problems, behavioural problems and language problems.

There are some excellent publications available specifically about learning difficulties (see the Resources section at the end of the book) so I have decided to restrict my discussion to how learning difficulties affect communication. Perhaps the best way to do this is to describe a typical learning-disabled patient.

Damien is twelve and there is a history of learning difficulties in his family. He finds it hard to keep still and appears to be in perpetual motion. Because his comprehension of lengthy and complex instruction is poor he is forever carrying out the wrong instruction in the wrong place at the wrong time. However, he shows little awareness of this difficulty, and impulsively carries out any task given to him.

In the classroom Damien has been labelled the class clown and he is always disturbing others with his constant chatter and movement. His behaviour is more like that of an eight-year-old. His conversation is rapid, punctuated by moments when he stops and struggles for the correct word. He tends to go off at tangents so that the listener becomes totally confused. He shows no insight into jokes or stories with a moral, and tends to take everything literally, for example, interpreting 'You drive me up the wall' as just that: a car driving up a wall.

Damien does, however, possess a delightful, quirky quality which makes him very lovable. He always has an opinion about everything and views his learning problems with a sense of humour. His bright attitude to his difficulties means that his self-esteem is high and he copes well with life in general, unlike many learning-disabled children, whose condition makes them miserable. Damien's memory of past events is excellent, but his short-term memory is poor. The grammatical structure of his sentences is poor and his sentences often don't make sense. He has great difficulty in reading, spelling and writing and will avoid any of these tasks if he can. He cannot recite the days of the week or the months of the year, does not know his left from his right and has difficulty telling the time or saying the alphabet.

Some readers may by now have recognised some of Damien's qualities as part of their own child's personality makeup. In more structured terms the difficulties which I have described are:

- Short attention span
- Difficulty in keeping still
- Auditory memory problems (difficulty remembering information that is given verbally)
- Short-term memory problems

- Word-finding problems (difficulty in remembering a particular word)
- Auditory perception difficulties (problems differentiating one sound from another)
- Poor comprehension skills, particularly of lengthy or complex instructions
- Problems with left/right orientation
- Difficulty in telling the time and understanding past, present and future tenses
- Difficulty with series of words such as the days of the week and months of the year
- Poor general language skills
- Difficulty in constructing grammatically correct sentences
- Lack of awareness of own behaviour and therefore an inability to gauge its appropriateness
- Impulsiveness
- No continuity of thought in general conversation
- Poor reading, spelling and writing skills
- A strong tendency to take things literally and a poor grasp of jokes
- Immature behaviour

What to do if your child has a problem

If you feel that your child is intelligent but is not progressing in school as he should, there is a chance that he is learning disabled. Often the clue towards discovering this is the child's frustration at his own lack of progress and general difficulties. Once you decide to have this investigated, I would recommend the following course of action.

The first step is to have your child assessed by his school counsellor, but you may have to wait for a while before he can be seen. If you aren't prepared to wait you can seek an independent assessment from an educational psychologist. This will probably be quite expensive. An educational psychologist will be able to tell you how your child stands amongst children in his grade and how he is progressing in such areas as spelling, reading and maths.

You could then take your child to be assessed by a developmental optometrist, who will evaluate how your child uses his eyes to read. Often vision can be normal but eye use can be poor. If you are concerned about your child's balance or coordination you may wish to seek out the help of a paediatric physiotherapist. Difficulties with fine motor skills such as gripping small objects, which would make writing difficult, should be dealt with by an occupational therapist.

Among these various professionals you should certainly see a speech pathologist to have the child's memory, auditory skills and language skills assessed. A speech pathologist will also be able to comment knowledgeably on all of the symptoms described above.

There are many alternative treatments for learning difficulties also available, such as the wearing of coloured glasses and elimination diets. I have no bias for or against such treatment, as I have had patients for whom these alternatives have succeeded and others for whom they have failed. Many parents will only turn to the use of drugs in treatment as a last resort, if at all. Again, I have seen patients who have responded to drug therapy and others who have not. My advice is to use whatever works for each individual child.

As I have said before, as a parent you know your child better than anyone else, so trust your own instincts to choose what is right for your child, basing your decisions on the professional advice that you receive.

KEY POINTS

- Speech pathologists can diagnose and treat many of the problems associated with learning difficulties.
- Some of the obvious signs of a learning problem include a limited attention span, short-term memory problems and difficulties with many areas of language and communication.
- If you feel that your child has a problem you could start by seeing the school counsellor or an educational psychologist.
- There are many alternative treatments available, and each child will respond differently to the various forms of treatment.

Chapter Ten

STIMULATING NORMAL LANGUAGE DEVELOPMENT

This section provides you with specific ideas for stimulating your child's communication skills from birth to five years of age. It is not only for parents, but for teachers, babysitters, grandparents and all caregivers.

Chapter 11 will deal specifically with helping your child if he has communication difficulties.

Birth to six months

Giving your baby speech stimulation can be pure joy or pure embarrassment. Some parents don't mind making strange noises at their baby, while others feel silly. But whether you are comfortable with it or not, early intervention is the key to helping your child develop normal communication skills.

Holding your baby in your arms and talking to him is a very important part of parent-child bonding. It is also the first step towards stimulating healthy speech. Some parents do this automatically but others don't see the point in talking to someone who can't talk back. However, if you are persistent in providing stimulation for your baby you will soon discover him responding in many ways.

The first step in stimulating your baby is to enable him to listen to a large range of different environmental noises and speech sounds. Begin by using toys that make noises, such as a small drum, a rattle or a squeaky toy. Expose him to a wide variety of these noises. In a similar way it's important to expose him to a variety of speech noises. Begin with tongue movements and funny sounds: blow raspberries, stick out your tongue and wiggle it about. Move on to speech sounds: make lip noises such as /p, b, w, m/ over and over again. These sounds can be easily seen on the mouth and are therefore the easiest for your baby to copy. If he doesn't copy what you do, don't despair, just keep on working on the stimulation and try to be patient.

To draw your baby's attention to your mouth you can hold up a small toy next to your mouth as you say the sound. You can also make the toy jump along the ground and say the noise over and over. For example the ball might bounce on the ground as you say 'b b b b'. The teddy might jump along the edge of the cot as you say 'm m m m'.

Another important part of speech stimulation is to respond to every sound your baby makes by hugs and smiles and by trying to copy him. He will soon understand that he can change his environment through communication. Sometimes it can be difficult to imitate the exact sound that your baby makes, as he is capable of making every sound in every language. It is your model which allows him to eventually focus in on English or whatever language you speak at home.

You may have noticed that your baby is very vocal during or immediately after he's been fed. Take advantage of the situation and do your speech stimulation after each meal.

Ask everyone that spends a significant amount of time with your baby to talk to him constantly and make speech and non-speech sounds.

It may take a little while before your baby starts to copy the sounds that you make, so this will require a degree of patience. However, the day he looks you straight in the eye and says 'mu' for 'mum' or 'da' for 'dad' you will be rewarded for your efforts.

It's important to remember that when children first begin to speak they do not sound like adults. That is to say, they may say 'bo' for 'bottle' and 'bu' for 'baby'. Sometimes parents are listening for an adult speech model and don't realise their baby is communicating with them.

Six to twelve months

We already know that between approximately six and nine months your baby will start to babble. It is at this stage that you will begin to hear the sing-song quality of adult speech. The development of intonation can be a great source of entertainment for brothers and sisters as well as parents. Try to copy every attempt at babbling and the intonation patterns, even if you can't imitate them exactly. Also make sure that you reward your child for his communication attempts with hugs and smiles.

Between about nine and twelve months your baby will start to combine nonsense words in jargoning. He will also enjoy playing turn-taking games such as 'peek-a-boo' which help to develop the turn-taking skills that occur when people have a conversation. They are an important part of language development.

Remember that your child may continue to jargon even once he has started developing single words. Continue to be patient, give him time to say what he needs to say and let him know that what he says is important, even if it does sound like a foreign language keep trying to copy his jargoning, even if it is difficult. You may be surprised to hear an older sibling copying this 'foreign language' exactly, and they may even be able to interpret it!

Once your child starts to use single words he will have developed a great many communication skills. He is no longer a baby but a very skilled individual. His sounds will now develop in an ordered pattern and the errors that he makes will be consistent. For example he may say /t/ for /k/ and therefore 'tup' for 'cup' or /g/ for /d/ and therefore 'guck' for 'duck'.

These are normal behaviours for the child mastering single words. If you take the time and have the patience to stimulate your child's speech a little each day you will be richly rewarded.

Twelve to eighteen months

Talk slowly and clearly to your child to provide him with a good speech model. Repeat any difficult words for him, and use gestures to aid his comprehension. Constantly discuss with him what you are doing and encourage him to describe what he's doing. Make every talking activity fun. Show him that he can change the world around him by communicating with others. Discourage other family members from talking *for* him. Expand on the sentences that your child makes to provide him with a good model for more complex language, for example, if he says 'blue truck' say: 'Yes, that's a big blue truck. It's your blue truck'. Play games asking the child to follow simple instructions such as: 'Touch your toes, touch your nose, point to the door, point to your shirt'. Provide the child with three or four toys and ask him to hand you certain ones, for example, 'Give me the pig. Give me the duck'. Look through all sorts of bright and colourful books with him, encouraging him to point to objects and activities as you name them. Look through your child's toy box with him, discussing the function of each object, for example, 'Cup: we drink with a cup. Spoon: we eat with a spoon'. Watch children's television shows with your child as they provide excellent ideas for craft, cooking and play activities, all of which can be talked about as you do them together during and after the show. Make a scrapbook and paste in all sorts of bright pictures, adding to this each day. This will encourage development of vocabulary.

Eighteen months to two years

Listen patiently to what your child says, copying the sentences that he produces and expanding on them. Give him the time and space that he needs to communicate with you. Remember to reinforce his language attempts with lots of smiles and hugs. Help him to learn new words each day by adding pictures to your scrapbook and by naming everything you come in contact with: 'door, sky, bird, tree'. It doesn't matter what it is, *name it*. Take your child on excursions to the beach, to the zoo, on a train, on a ferry. Discuss what you will be doing before you go, then discuss what you did and what you saw when you return home. If your child uses the wrong sound or wrong word for something, simply repeat the correct form for him. Don't criticise his attempts to communicate. Keep everything positive.

Two years

At this age you can begin to ask your child numerous questions to stimulate his language. Continue to read books and discuss family outings both before and after the event. Continue to take advantage of the children's shows on television and make sure that you talk *with* your child rather than *at* him. Talk about what you are doing and what he's doing. Talk about how you're feeling and how he's feeling. Remember to copy and extend his sentences. Provide lots of positive feedback when he says a three-word sentence on his own. Continue to extend his vocabulary by using the scrapbook and by looking at books and discovering new words. Simple picture dictionaries are particularly useful.

Three years

Often at this age children repeat their words over and over. This is also the age when stuttering may develop, so be aware of repetitions, especially those accompanied by any tension or embarrassment. Have your child assessed by a speech pathologist if you are concerned about his speech. The speech pathologist will be able to tell you if your child is stuttering, or going through a normal stage in speech and language development. Continue to talk to your child, extending his sentences and his knowledge of the world in general. Go out of your way to introduce him to new and interesting situations. Begin to read longer stories to your child and include those with more imaginary aspects. Make him aware of similarities and differences between things. For example, 'This glass is full. This glass is empty. This block is big. This block is little'. Encourage your child to ask lots of questions.

Four years

At four years of age your child's sentences will be longer and more complex. He should have mastered many aspects of grammar. Remember that grammar includes the sound system, meaning system, word system and word order system of language. Helping your child to classify objects or pictures according to their categories is a good activity at this age. For example, he can sort pictures into piles of food and drink, or hot and cold things. Give him more responsibility in family matters by allowing him to help in the planning of outings, or decide what you will prepare for dinner. Remember that your child's speech and his language will still have some errors, but you should be able to understand at least 80 per cent of what he says. When he produces a sound or language error, provide him with the correct form and ask him to repeat it after you, but don't pressure him if he doesn't wish to cooperate. It is important to maintain language as a positive experience.

Five years

By five years of age your child will have developed almost all aspects of his language. He should now be a highly efficient speaker but will still understand more than he is able to say, that is, his competence will exceed his performance. Now you can ask him to tell you a story at bedtime. Quiz him about basic colours and numbers. Look through magazines and books together and discuss what is happening in them. Try to ask open-ended questions like 'What's happening here?' to encourage maximum use of language. Urge your child to commit short songs and rhymes to memory. Continue classifying pictures into categories and begin to discuss the concepts of past and future tense, giving examples of each to clarify the meaning. Use family outings to reinforce these time concepts by discussing future plans and activities in the past. Most of all remember to talk to your child now as you would to an adult. Never talk down to him.

Ten golden rules for working with your child

Here are ten basic guidelines to help you start working with your child in the most efficient and simple way. They apply to all aspects of communication work, both assessment and stimulation. They are only guidelines, so feel free to add your own creative ideas. Use what you know about your child to best advantage. It's important to have confidence in your own ability to carry out these tasks, and to have some fun while doing so.

1　Choose a quiet environment. If your child is of school age then sit him at a desk. If he is a preschooler then give him the choice to work at a small desk or on the floor. Babies can be stimulated in their crib or in any position where they have good eye contact with you. Don't work where other children are busy playing, watching television or working. Make it clear to other family members that you are not to be disturbed.

2　Find a time that suits both of you. Don't try to work together when you are about to serve up dinner, or in the car on the way to school, or when his favourite television program is on. Nor would I advise waking a baby or toddler to work with him, as tears or a tantrum are a likely outcome.

3　When performing the stimulation activities, work for ten to twenty minutes each day. Don't try to do the entire week's allocation of activities in a single sitting, as you are both likely to end up feeling frustrated. The secret is to do a little bit each day. It's also important to think seriously about what sort of behaviour you consider reasonable for your child in this situation. I have found that many parents become strict taskmasters who hardly allow their children to breathe when they start working with them. Expect a certain amount of fidgeting, but rule out swinging from the rafters.

4 If your child has difficulty in sitting still for a twenty-minute session, you may wish to make a contract with him so that he works for ten minutes, plays for five minutes, then works for another ten minutes.

5 Try to make each small session different, fun and full of varying activities. This isn't as difficult as it sounds if you use some simple games and attention-holding rewards, but make sure that the games don't interfere too much with the work at hand. Look upon each game as an extra activity aimed at keeping the child interested in the work.

Some children will work well without any games and are more than happy to work for a smile or a hug, or verbal praise.

6 You may wish to use a variety of rewards, such as stickers, stamps, stars and balloons, or even a large reward when the child has made a marked improvement. It is important to choose a reward to work towards that the child really likes. By doing this you can head off all sorts of difficulties.

7 Always give specific feedback to your child about his work. Try also to make a habit of giving feedback on every single word or sound that your child makes within the working period. For example you might say: 'That was a good /s/ sound' or 'That was a good try, now have another go and remember to make a little bit of air come out on the /s/ sound.' This will provide him with plenty of specific ways to improve his talking on his next attempt. If you forget to give the child feedback, remind yourself to do it on the next occasion, and keep reminding yourself until it becomes second nature. Don't be surprised if you suddenly wake up at

2 a.m., sit bolt upright in bed and murmur 'good /s/ sound' to your spouse! These habits have a way of working themselves into every corner of our lives.

8 Avoid allowing other children in the family to correct your little worker's speech, because it can cause him great frustration. It is better to make it mum's or dad's task for the month.

9 Try to be aware of the tendency to want immediate results. It is difficult not to be pushy when good results mean so much to you, but from my experience it is those parents who keep a sense of objectivity and work at a steady pace who achieve the best results.

10 Involve other caregivers as much as possible, and do all you can to make them part of the process. The important thing is to teach the other person to do the work exactly the way you do it so that there is consistency of purpose and procedure, otherwise the child can become confused. The best way to achieve this is to explain to the person what to do and then demonstrate it for them step-by-step. If you feel happy to do so, ask the caregiver to watch a number of your work sessions with your child before embarking on their own. This should clear up any misunderstandings and give them the confidence they may need to begin.

When behaviour gets in the way

It may sometimes be difficult to get your child to cooperate with you and do the necessary work. Some children, especially the very young, have difficulty sitting at a table for any period of time to work. Often children find it difficult to pay attention for lengthy periods of time. You may be lucky and have an angel to work with, but for those of you who don't, when the work just has to be done you need to know the most appropriate way to cope.

If you find it hard to get your child to imitate what you say when you first begin, try a different tack and ask him to copy actions that you make such as putting your hands on your head or touching your nose. Turn what you are doing into a game. Once you have his full cooperation for these physical tasks, you can then introduce some verbal tasks.

When dealing with children and their behaviour it is always a good idea to try to catch them doing the correct thing, whether it be sitting still, looking in the mirror, or simply being pleasant to little sister, and praising or rewarding them for it. Usually, however, it is easier to catch them doing the wrong thing so you need to have a few tricks and strategies up your sleeve to help you hang on to your sanity. Let's look at this area more closely.

Discipline

Discipline isn't a dirty word. When working with children discipline can be a very positive learning experience. Unfortunately many people think of discipline only as physical punishment — yelling, screaming and hitting. Discipline doesn't have to be like this: there are other options.

Physical punishment doesn't work. Even though it stops the child from doing the wrong thing it doesn't teach him what type of behaviour is expected instead. It makes both the child and the parent feel bad. The child may become fearful and angry and, in some cases, children have been known to take out their anger on younger children or the family pets.

From my experience, it is very difficult for most parents to ignore their child's poor or inappropriate behaviour, although there is the occasional parent who is happy to watch their toddler grind cream cake into the carpet or swear persistently at the cat. There are some behaviours that can be reduced by merely ignoring them, if you can, such as clowning around, sillyness, face-pulling and swearing. The most important thing about ignoring your child's behaviour is to be consistent and not give in. If you give in, your child learns that if he keeps the bad behaviour up long enough he will get what he wants. It usually takes about two or three days of ignoring the bad behaviour before it is reduced. This is a technique for those of you who are gentle of heart and as patient as a saint.

Time out

The most appropriate technique to use when your child flatly refuses to work (or to respond to any other request) is called 'time out'. It involves removing the child from a rewarding situation, that is, from a situation where they have your attention. Set aside a special time out area away from all the family action and anything interesting or fun to play with (reinforcers). It should be a boring room like the toilet or the laundry (with all toxic substances well out of reach). The child's bedroom is a poor choice because there will be many toys, books and other interesting things to occupy their time. You can then explain to your child that he will be sent to the time out area every time he refuses to do what is asked of him.

On the next occasion that your child refuses to do what he is asked, simply take him gently and calmly to the time out area and

set the alarm on the clock for two or three minutes. Don't lecture him or get angry. When the time is up, bring him back to the work area where all of the reinforcers are, and state your request once again. If he refuses to comply then repeat the time out procedure. Even if you initially have to do this two or three times, it is well worth the effort in the long run.

Time out should never be used as a means for parents to get a few moments peace. It also isn't designed to scare your child. It is a specific punishment technique that should only be given in the manner outlined.

Time out can be particularly helpful if your child is a master at getting out of doing his work. He may use one or a combination of the following ploys:
'I want to go to the toilet.' (The most common ploy and one you can't afford to dismiss.)
'My tongue/mouth/teeth, etc. hurt.'
'I want a drink.'
'I'm missing out on my favourite television program/sports practice, etc. when I'm here.'

He may climb under the desk, over the desk and even out of the window. (You may be saving money on speech therapy bills but you will be making up for them in hospital bills.)

This is where being both the parent and the 'talking helper' is quite an advantage as you know your child's favourite games, rewards, and ploys for avoiding work. Arm yourself with a time out area and forge ahead.

THE OUTSIDE ANGEL SYNDROME
The 'outside angel' syndrome is a common phenomenon. If you find that your child is an angel with everybody else and a devil

with you then you may wish to ask someone else to work with him. Do make sure that you explain everything to the helper involved. Preferably have them read this book.

If a number of people are working with the one child, for example mother, grandmother and preschool teacher, it is vital that they don't confuse him. Their approach to both the work and behaviour standards needs to be consistent.

Key points

- The key to helping your child develop normal communication skills and overcome problems is early intervention.
- The basic rule for stimulating your child's language at any age is to be encouraging and support all attempts at communicating.
- Always try to make language stimulation fun and interesting.
- If your child's behaviour is a problem when you are working, try using the 'time out' technique.

Chapter Eleven

HELPING CHILDREN WITH PROBLEMS

How to get a non-talker to talk

We have now come to the tricky but exciting area of language stimulation for a non-talker. The learning of language is such a complex activity, that sometimes providing a stimulating environment full of rewards is just not enough to help a child form his first words.

First words usually emerge between approximately twelve and eighteen months, and there is great debate among health professionals as to when advice should be sought if the child doesn't develop his single words during this period. As I have already made clear, I am a firm believer in early intervention. Too many doctors advise parents to wait until their child starts school before seeking professional help. By the age of five a child has almost completed his entire language development. So 'wait until he starts school' or 'just wait a little longer' can be very dangerous advice indeed.

Often parents know that their child understands everything that is said but he just won't talk. This is the parents' definition of 'frustration'!

There are three crucial steps to stimulating language in children with normal understanding, but limited verbal skills. The first step is to modify your own language. You need to talk to your child at or just above the level of language he is or should be using. If you want him to start using single words you should talk to him in single words and allow him to focus on these instead of confusing him with lengthy sentences. If you want him to use two-word combinations, which normally develop between eighteen months and two years of age, then you need to talk to him in two- or three-word combinations.

The second step concerns your entire family. You need, as a family, to set up 'a talking environment,' an environment where there are rewards for attempts at communication. Sometimes the youngest child is slow to develop language because the older children and parents anticipate his every requirement and he thus has no need to communicate. In some cases, you should withhold something that your child wants until he makes some attempt, any attempt, at saying the word.

Naturally, individual consideration is needed. No-one knows better than you where your child's limits lie and at what point he will throw a tantrum. In some cases it's worth a few tears to just start the child off on the road to talking. Of course every attempt, no matter how small, should be rewarded immediately.

The third step is to perform direct language stimulation in a structured way working specifically towards particular language goals.

Now let's look more closely at these three steps, and end with some tips for more general language stimulation.

Modifying your own language

Modifying your own language is the first step in stimulating language in your child. Begin by choosing a particular time of day such as bathtime or lunchtime to practise cutting down your language.

If your child is talking mostly in single words and you want to develop two-word combinations, then talk to him using only two-word combinations. At lunchtime say: 'Here lunch'; 'Here food'; 'Here drink'; 'Robby drink?'; 'More drink?' and so on. If you find yourself slipping into full sentences then simply go back and repeat the sentence in the two-word form, for example, 'Come and sit down, it's lunchtime' becomes 'Robby sit. Eat lunch'. Similarly, at bathtime you can say things like: 'Robby's bath'; 'Sit bath'; 'Where soap?' 'Here soap'; 'Robby wash'; 'Wash face'; 'Wash toes' and so on.

When you become used to doing this in one situation then extend your repertoire to other situations. If other parents ask you why you are talking to your child in 'baby talk' simply explain to them that you are not using baby talk but rather stimulating his language at the correct level.

Some parents automatically cut down their language when they talk to their children. For others it may take a great deal of practice in a variety of situations before it becomes an automatic process.

'A talking environment'

The perfect talking environment is one where you, as parents, encourage and reward your child for any attempt he makes at communication. It includes the following:

- Encouraging your child to make any attempt at a word before he is given the item that he wants.
- Clapping your hands and looking very pleased at every attempt he makes to communicate.
- Making sure you don't ignore any attempt at communication.
- Not pushing your child into saying the word like you do.
- Preventing brothers and sisters from talking for your child but encouraging them to help with the talking project at hand.

Direct language stimulation

The third aspect of language stimulation involves hands-on stimulation at least three times a week in a structured way. The following activities are recommended for those of you who don't have a trained professional treating your child and who have a non-verbal child or a child who is using only a few single words when he should be using more.

- Sit on the floor or at a table with a box of toys. Don't allow the child to touch the toybox as you will be using the toys one at a time to work with.

  Choose a toy or a familiar object such as a cup or a spoon and hold it up in front of your child. When you have his attention say the name of the object three times. Encourage him to repeat the word (any attempt will do at this stage). If he responds then give him a reward — a hug, a smile, or a sticker on the hand for example. Choose a few items and keep working on these for as long as is necessary. Then move on to words in the following categories: common household objects; people; clothes; animals; body parts.

  If your child won't copy any of the words that you present him with then try getting him to do physical movements on request, as I mentioned earlier, such as putting his hands up in the air, touching his toes and so on. If this doesn't work, demonstrate the action yourself and then ask the child to follow. Once he has joined in, introduce the talking tasks once again, and you may be more successful.

- Whenever your child says a single word, expand it to two words, for example, if he said 'cup' you might say 'big cup', or show him another cup and say 'more cup' or hide the cup and say 'no cup'. This exercise will help to expand his vocabulary.

- Give your child choices before giving him something. Instead of just giving him a drink, for example, ask: 'juice? milk?', and encourage him to say which he wants.

- Label everything that your child comes into contact with throughout the day. For example, label the spoon, dish and cup for when he is eating or objects in the bath like soap, duck and water.

If you have been seriously working on the activities mentioned above, including the direct language stimulation, and making no progress, it is important that you seek the help of a trained speech pathologist. It may only take a few visits to the speech pathologist before your child starts cooperating with you at home. Be aware, however, that it does take a good deal of patience to perform any or all of the above procedures, so take it slowly — you could even give yourself rewards along the way!

General language stimulation

There are many general tasks that can be done to help stimulate language development.

Talk slowly and simply to your child. Look at him when you talk to him and try not to use 'baby talk' like 'choo choo' for train and 'nana' for banana. Before, during and after your child is introduced to a new situation, talk about it. Talk about what it will be like to go to the zoo. Discuss what you might see there. When you get home discuss what happened and what you saw. You can do this for almost any everyday experience, like going shopping, going for a walk, or even cleaning the house. Whatever you experience together, talk about it. When your child talks to you, listen. Praise him for his talking and be enthusiastic. Repeat what he says and add to it, for example, if he says: 'car', say: 'Yes, that's a big red car'. If he says 'drink' say: 'You want a drink'. This confirms that you've understood what he's said and provides him with a good model of how to expand his sentences.

For a child aged between three and seven you can also encourage talking by using the following activities.

- Make up talking games built upon the nursery rhymes and songs you know and that you hear on television.

- Discuss the child's favourite television programs and what happens in them.

- Play memory games such as the shopping game. You start by saying 'I went to the shop and I bought (say) some eggs,' and then your child repeats what you have said, and adds an item that he has thought of. You then repeat what he has said, adding a further item, and so the game continues.

- Discuss what you would need to take with you on a trip to the beach, on a picnic or to the snow, and so on.

- Play games to see who can think of the most items in a category, for example food, drink or animals.

- Discuss everything you have done since you woke up in the morning.

- Talk about a video or a movie that you and your child have watched recently.

- Make up a story using finger or hand puppets.

- Talk about the function of different objects, such as scissors, egg beaters, pencils, and so on.
- Play 'I spy with my little eye something beginning with the sound . . .'

How to help a child with an articulation problem

The information that follows is a simplified formula for working on your child's speech sounds. Each step in the process is explained below and then summarised in Table 4 (page 118). You may use Table 4 as a ready reckoner by sticking it on the fridge door or in the front of a book you compile to be your child's speech workbook.

From your assessment list of error sounds (found through following the steps in Chapter 3) choose a consonant to work on. We will call this the target sound. It is best to start work on a sound for which the articulation can be easily seen by the child, such as lip sounds, for example /p, b, w, m/, and tongue on the teeth sounds, for example /t, d, l, n/. Do not work with vowel sounds as these are difficult and require professional assistance. Blends (two consonants together like /pl/ in 'plane') should only be worked on once the child has achieved accurate usage of each individual sound.

Step 1: sound on its own

Ask your child to say the target sound after you ten times. Remember to give him plenty of encouragement. Get him to look at your mouth or at his own mouth in a small stand-up mirror as the sound is said. Each time he tries the sound give him some feedback, for example 'That was a good /p/ sound, you made lots of air come out of your mouth' or 'Good try, but we need more air to come out. Try to feel the air on your hand like I do.' (Hold your hand up and feel the air as you say the /p/ sound to demonstrate.) To determine what form of feedback to give for a particular sound turn to the section at the end of this chapter entitled 'Specific Feedback for Individual Sounds'.

Keep a score in your child's speech workbook of his attempts at the sound. If he gets eight or more out of ten correct then go on to the next step. If he gets less than eight correct then try Step 1 again. Remember to give instructions and feedback for every attempt. On some occasions you will find that your child fails to produce the target sound even after many attempts. If this happens it is wise to move on to another sound to avoid frustration.

Step 2: sound in nonsense words

Now let's work on the sound in different positions in words. It is usually best to work on the sound first at the front of the word, then at the end of the word, and finally in the middle of the word.

Ask your child to say the following nonsense words after you. I will use the target sound /p/ here as an example.

pah pee poo pay paw pow poh pa pe pi

You can use virtually any combination here as long as it's your target sound followed by a vowel.

If we were working on /p/ at the ends of words then the nonsense words would look like this:

ahp eep oop ayp owp ohp ap ep ip

If we were working on /p/ in the middle of words the nonsense words would look like this:

ahpah eepee oopoo aypay owpow ohpoh apa epe ipi

If your child gets eight or more out of ten correct then continue on to Step 3. If his score is less than eight then repeat Step 2, or go back to Step 1 if he's having a lot of trouble.

Remember to be patient. It can take some children two to three weeks to master a sound in nonsense words. The golden rule is a little each day and loads of encouragement for both yourself and your child.

Step 3: sound in single words

PART 1

Now we work with the sound in real words. At this point you need to find ten simple pictures of things whose names begin with the target sound. (This is if you are working on the sound at the front of the word.) Try to avoid pictures of things whose names include the substitution sound that your child uses for the target sound. For example, if your child says /t/ for /k/, try and avoid pictures of a cat or a kite because they have the substitution sound /t/ in them.

Also try to avoid pictures of things whose names have consonant blends in them, such as /fl, bl, tr, dr, kr/. For example, if you're working on the sound /p/ don't use a picture of a plane. (A child should be able to correctly produce the two sounds separately in conversation before attempting blends.)

Ask your child to repeat this list of target words after you. Give instructions and make him look in the mirror or at your mouth. Remember to give him feedback after every attempt. Don't wait until he's said all ten words, as that won't help him at all. If he scores eight or more then go on to the second part of Step 3.

PART 2
Now get your child to say the words on his own as you point to the pictures. Again give him specific feedback all the way through.

If he scores eight or more then go on to Step 4. If his score is less than eight then repeat the second half of Step 3.

Step 4: using a carrier phrase

A carrier phrase is a phrase that is used over and over again, with the relevant word tacked onto the end, for example 'I like pens.' 'I like paints.' 'I like puppies.' If the phrase doesn't always make sense when the word is added on, don't worry.

Continue to use the ten simple pictures that you found for Step 3. You can add to these, of course, and change them so that your child doesn't become bored with the same old material.

Choose your phrase, such as 'I like . . . ' and add on each of the ten words. Ask your child to say each one after you, giving him specific feedback each time, for example, 'I like pizza'. If he scores eight or more out of ten you may then wish him to do the phrases on his own, but this isn't essential. If his score is below eight then go back to Step 3 or simply repeat Step 4.

Step 5: sound in sentences

PART 1
Now take the simple pictures and make up ten simple short sentences with each one. Ask your child to repeat each sentence after you and give specific feedback. If he gets eight out of ten right then go on to the second half of Step 5. If not, repeat this step or go back to Step 4.

PART 2
Now let your child make up each sentence. Make sure that he keeps the sentence simple and discourage him from using words that include his error sound. Give him feedback after each sentence. If he scores eight or more out of ten then move on to Step 6. If he does not do so well then repeat the second half of Step 5.

Step 6: sound in stories

PART 1
Using all ten pictures now make up a silly story. If we were to make up a story for the sound /k/ at the front of the word, it might go something like this:

This is a story about a cow. He woke up in the morning and gave his mother a kiss. For breakfast he ate some carrots and some cake. He had a cup of coffee. Then he picked up his keys and jumped in the car. He went to visit his friend the king who lives in a castle. The king had a cough and a cold.

Tell your child the story up to three times until he's familiar with it. Then tell the story and get your child to fill in the gaps, pointing to the pictures as you go.

This is a story about a . . . He woke up in the morning and gave his mother a . . . , and so on.

It is very important to give your child feedback on each word in the story immediately he has said it. Don't wait until the end of the story. If your child gets eight or more out of ten correct then go on to the second half of Step 6. If he does not do so well, repeat the first half of Step 6.

PART 2

Ask your child to tell your story all on his own this time. If he is very keen he can make up his own, but he must use the pictures and not wander off the track. Give him specific feedback as he goes. If he scores eight or more out of ten then go on to Step 7. If he is less successful, repeat the second half of Step 6.

Step 7: sound in conversation

Now we make the huge leap into conversational speech. Until this point it is a good idea not to correct your child's target sound in his conversational speech. Only correct him at the level that he is at, for example, at single sentence level.

Now there is a greater focus than ever upon your input. Be particularly patient with yourself and your child at this point, or you may become frustrated.

Choosing a specific time of the day, like bathtime, lunchtime or dinnertime, then at this time tell your child that you will be listening for his good target sound, for example: 'Good /k/ sound'.

Listen carefully in conversation and every time your child says a good target sound all on his own, first time, reward him immediately. (See the section entitled 'Carryover of good sounds into every-day talking' at the end of this chapter for reward ideas.)

You may find that at the beginning you have to almost trick your child into saying a word with the target sound in it, for example, by asking a question like, 'What did we eat for your birthday?' With luck the answer will be 'cake'.

Focus only on the target sound and only on that sound in its position in the word, so if you're working on /k/ at the front of the word, don't spend time correcting /k/ at the end of the word, or any other sound that is in error.

Then start to practise this procedure at different times of the day. After a while you will be able to hear the sound while you are concentrating on something else, like making dinner, watching television, doing the laundry or balancing the household accounts. It simply takes practice.

By monitoring your child's speech in this way you are helping to establish the target sound as the new and correct sound. Soon he will be correcting his own attempts and after that it should become an automatic process for him as well.

This process is usually pretty demanding. More time is needed to achieve the successful carryover of the target sound into conversation than for the successful completion of any of the other steps.

Encourage others such as grandparents or teachers to also listen for the target sound. Avoid allowing siblings to correct your child's attempts as this can lead to major family brawls.

TABLE 4

HOW TO WORK ON INDIVIDUAL SOUNDS

Target	Method	Example
1 Sound on its own	Part 1: Repeat sound after you * Part 2: On his own	/p/
2 Sound in nonsense words Front Middle End	 Repeat after you Repeat after you Repeat after you	 pah, pee eep, oop oopoo, aypay
3 Sound in single words	Part 1: Repeat after you Part 2: On his own	pies, paint
4 Using a carrier phrase	Repeat after you	I like . . . I like pies I like paints
5 Sound in sentences	Part 1: Repeat after you Part 2: On his own	My mum makes pies
6 Sound in stories	Part 1: After listening he fills in the gaps Part 2: Tells the story on his own	Make up a silly story using /p/
7 Sound in conversation	Feedback every time sound is used	Listen for /p/

* YOUR CHILD SHOULD BE ACHIEVING AN 80 PER CENT SUCCESS RATE BEFORE MOVING ON TO THE NEXT STEP.

Specific feedback for individual sounds

Below you will find a list of feedback instructions that you can give your child for individual target sounds. Remember that we are dealing with consonants and blends (two consonant sounds blended together, for example /fl/ as in 'flag').

If you're working on a blend you will probably find that only one consonant in the blend is said incorrectly. For this reason the feedback for the target sound to be blended will be the same as for the single consonant.

If one part of the instruction seems to work better than the others then use just the most effective one. When you're dealing with a sound from the list where air needs to be blown from the mouth, as soon as your child can make the sound correctly without holding up his hand to feel the air, drop the instruction to use his hand.

/p/   Lips together. Make the air come out. Feel the air on your hand.

/b/   Lips together. No air comes out. Make a big popping noise in your mouth.

/w/   Lips together. Push your lips forward.

/m/   Lips together. No air comes out. Feel the buzzing noise on the side of your nose.

/h/   Make a noise like a puppy dog panting. Make the air come out. Feel the air on your hand.

/ng/   Make the back of your tongue jump up in the back of your mouth. Feel the buzzing noise on your nose.

/n/   Put the tip of your tongue up behind your top teeth. Feel the buzzing noise on your nose.

/t/   Put the tip of your tongue up behind your top teeth. Make the air come out. Feel the air on your hand.

/d/ Put the tip of your tongue up behind your top teeth. No air comes out. Feel the buzzing noise by putting your hand on your throat.

/y/ Put the tip of your tongue down behind your bottom teeth. Make the sides of your tongue jump up and touch your top teeth.

/k/ Make the back of your tongue jump up. Make the air come out. Feel the air on your hand.

/g/ Make the back of your tongue jump up. No air comes out. Feel the buzzing noise by putting your hand on your throat.

/f/ Bite your bottom lip gently. Make the air come out. Feel the air on your hand.

/v/ Bite your bottom lip gently. No air comes out. Feel the buzzing noise by putting your hand on your throat.

/l/ Put the tip of your tongue up behind your top teeth. Don't let your lips do the work. Make your tongue do the work.

/sh/ Put the tip of your tongue up behind your top teeth. Put your teeth together. Make lots of air come out. It is a long sound. Feel the air on your hand.

/ch/ Put the tip of your tongue up behind your top teeth. Put your teeth together. Make lots of air come out in one big explosion. This is the sound that a train makes, ch ch ch.

/j/ Put the tip of your tongue up behind your top teeth. Put your teeth together. Make a big explosion in your mouth. Don't let any air come out. The word *jump* starts with this sound.

/s/ Put the tip of your tongue up behind your top teeth (or down behind your bottom teeth, depending which makes the better 's' sound.) Make a little bit of air come out. Feel the air on your hand.

/z/   Put the tip of your tongue up behind your top teeth (or down behind your bottom teeth). Make a buzzing noise on your teeth.

/r/   Curl your tongue up tight inside your mouth. Point it towards the back of your mouth. Make a roaring sound like a lion.

/th/   (As in 'thin'.) Put your tongue between your teeth. Make some air come out. Feel the air on your hand.

/th/   (As in 'this'.) Put your tongue between your teeth. Don't make any air come out. Make a buzzing noise. Feel the buzzing on your throat.

Carryover of good sounds into everyday talking

To assist your child in carrying over his target sound into his everyday talking you can try any one, all, or a number of the ideas below.

- Make your child a star chart. A good sound earns a star, 40 stars earns a prize.

- Make your child a stamp chart and use as above.

- Select a jar that can be filled with lollies or sultanas. For each attempt the child gets a lolly or a sultana to put in the jar. When the jar is full he may receive a prize plus the lollies.

- Use a tick chart. For each attempt your child gets a tick on his page. Ten ticks may result in a small prize.

- Form a contract with your child saying that you will give him a special toy when he fixes up his /k/ and /s/ sounds in his talking.

All sorts of variations can be made to these rewards and you as the parents will know what will or won't work with the child. Avoid being cajoled into promises of pets, BMX bikes, or holidays in Disneyland. Many children will work simply for a hug or a smile, but others will not. If your child adores prawns (I know one who does!) then use prawns as a reinforcer.

Another good idea to encourage carryover is to make up a large coloured poster involving a mixture of pictures with the target sound. Put this next to your star chart on the fridge door, in the bedroom, or in the rumpus room. Take it down every few days and look at it with your child. Play memory games, trying to remember what words start (or end, and so on) with your target sound.

Remember to focus on the little words that aren't always easy to draw or find pictures for. For example, your child will probably use the /k/ words 'can' and 'can't more often than any other /k/ words. You may wish to make a special day where you listen in conversation only for these words.

There is immense scope for carryover strategies, so have some fun being creative. This step often allows mums, parents and teachers to be kids again. Take advantage of it.

Games to play (or how to save your sanity)

In previous pages we have talked about the importance of making the work fun. Having a variety of games at your fingertips can make life much easier. For this purpose I am including here some of the tried and tested games that I've used with my patients over the years. They range from the most basic task to games that require a certain amount of effort.

- Draw ten circles. Each time the child attempts the target sound, he puts a string on a circle to make it a balloon. You can also put a stick onto the circle and make it into a lollipop. These can then be coloured-in after each attempt to say a word, phrase, or sentence.

- Play a snakes and ladders game. Each time your child attempts the target sound he gets to move—up the ladder if he is correct and down the snake if it was incorrect.

- Draw your child a racetrack game and divide it into squares. Write the words to be said in the squares. Roll a dice and move your button or toy car onto the correct square then say the word in the square that you land on. This can be used for single words, phrases, and sentences.

- The child throws a basketball or tennis ball into a bin from a set distance each time he correctly pronounces the target sound. This is a favourite with children who are very active.

- Have a picture hunt around the room for pictures you have set up which are of things that begin (or end, and so on) with the target sound. When a picture is found then the object depicted is named.

- Play a picture lotto game where you have two sets of pictures and you try to match them up. When the child matches two pictures he says the word, or phrase or sentence targeted.

- The child colours in a small part of a picture each time he attempts a task. Make the picture something that relates to the target sound. For example, for the sound /s/ draw a picture of a snake and call it 'Mr Snake'.

- Play a memory game with the child using a tray of objects whose names contain the target sound. Look at the objects for one or two minutes then cover them with a cloth. Try to remember which objects were on the tray.

- The child builds a block tower. Each time he says a target sound he adds another block to his tower.

- Make up two sets of picture cards for your child showing things named by the target words. Take turns in placing a card on the table until two cards that match appear. When the pictures match, the child has to put the word into a phrase or a sentence.

- The child matches a picture to the written target word from a choice of word cards that have been made by the parent. (This is for children who can read.) Every time the picture matches the written word then the sentence or word is said.

- Use a game of skittles and put the pictures of the target words onto the skittles with adhesive tape. When a skittle is knocked down the word or phrase or sentence is said.

These are only a few suggestions. The possibilities are endless. Why not make up your own games, with your child's help? Maybe you can adapt games stored away in the toy cupboard.

Key points

- If your child has normal understanding but limited verbal skills you need to modify your own language, set up a perfect talking environment in your home and work on direct language stimulation.
- Involve other family members and caregivers in providing a stimulating language environment, but don't allow siblings to correct a child's speech.
- If your child has an articulation problem, work in a structured wayon individual sounds and always give specific feedback.
- Always try to make the work as much fun as possible.

RESOURCES

This section contains a list of books to help you when working with your child and information about some organisations which provide speech pathology assistance.

Books for you

Babies! by Dr Christopher Green, Simon & Schuster, Sydney, 1988. Everything you need to know about baby's first year.

Babies Need Books by Dorothy Butler, Penguin, England, 1988. This beautifully written book highlights the joys of sharing reading activities with your child. It also lists suggested books for each age group.

Early Language: The Developing Child by husband and wife team Peter and Jill de Villiers, Fontana/Open Books, London, 1979. This book is also known with the title *Da-Da*. It is a comprehensive and slightly technical look at how babies develop speech and language. It is recommended reading for the enthusiast.

Games Games Games, the Education Department of South Australia, 1972. It includes reading, word recognition and listening activities galore. All are accompanied by great ideas for games.

The Good Book Guide to Children's Books, Penguin, England, 1984. This contains a selection of 600 recommended books for children.

The Hidden Handicap by Dr Gordon Serfontein, Simon & Schuster, Sydney, 1990. This is about helping children with learning difficulties, dyslexia and hyperactivity.

How to Help Your Child to Learn by Barbara Pheloung, Bantam-Tortoiseshell Books, 1988. An invaluable book concerning all aspects of learning difficulties.

100 First Words to Say with Your Baby by Edwina Riddell, Collins, Sydney, 1988. This book provides beautifully illustrated categories of your baby's first words.

Raising Kids O.K. by Dorothy Babcock and Terry Keepers, Avon Books, New York, 1977. This is a parent's guide to transactional analysis. It provides an interesting look at parenthood and would be a useful addition to your library.

The Read Aloud Handbook by Jim Trelease, Penguin, Ringwood, 1987. This has some very handy hints on reading aloud and contains a comprehensive book list of 300 stories, picture books and poetry books for children.

A Recipe for Effective Parenting by psychologists Petra McHugh and Sarah Evans, self-published, 1986. This provides no-nonsense guidelines for every aspect of behaviour and deals with the concept of time out. To obtain the book write directly to the authors at 60 King William Road, Goodwood, South Australia, 5034.

Useful Book: Songs and Ideas from Playschool, ABC Enterprises, Sydney, 1988. A wealth of language-stimulating activities based on stories, songs, fingerplays and craft activities for the preschooler.

The importance of books for your child

Many parents baulk at the idea of reading books to their babies, just as they baulk at the idea of performing talking stimulation activities with a seemingly unresponsive bundle of joy. However, many authors, educators and parents agree that books are an invaluable tool and should be introduced as early as when the baby first comes home from hospital.

A picture book is excellent at stimulating your child's speech and language. Most of the work is done for you. The book provides the material for discussion and opens the door to a myriad of language-promoting activities. When you are lost for language stimulating ideas, turn to a book for assistance.

Reading also provides an opportunity for closeness and sharing. A number of authors believe strongly in this bonding that occurs through the early introduction of books. They suggest that a relationship established through reading to one's child promotes closeness in the years that follow.

I am in full agreement with this theory, and believe that an early communication flow between parent and child will form a firm basis for later communication.

Many parents may feel intimidated by the thought of reading aloud to their child. They worry about making mistakes or not being interesting enough to hold their child's attention. I have no doubts that you will be pleasantly surprised at how accepting your child is of your mistakes. His main concern will be to maintain his personal time with you. Generally he will be a captive audience and will provide assistance when you come to a tricky patch.

It is no surprise that the child exposed to books as a

preschooler becomes a good reader at school, for by the time he is required to begin reading he will have had extensive experience of the written word and the complexities of grammar. By introducing books at an early age you will provide your child with the golden key to easily developed reading skills.

To help you choose appropriate books for your child, I am including a list of my favourite books for each age group. While only a guide, the list may help your child begin a marvellous journey with books that will last his entire life.

The first year

Two excellent books to begin with are Dick Bruna's *B is for Bear*, an alphabet book (Methuen), and *I Can Count*, a counting book (Methuen).

Two easy-to-use nursery rhyme books are *The Helen Oxenbury Nursery Rhyme Book* by Helen Oxenbury (Heinemann), and *Mother Goose's Nursery Rhymes* by Allen Atkinson (Bantam Books).

Lively and attractive board books are always a firm favourite and of these I personally favour *Little Spots* by Eric Hill (Heinemann), *Baby's Day* by Camilla Jessel (Methuen) and *Mog and Me* by Judith Kerr (Collins). A list of suitable picture books would go on for ever, but some of my favourites are *Are You There Bear?* by Ron Maris (Julia McRae), *Rosie's Walk* by Pat Hutchins (Puffin), *The Baby's Catalogue* by Janet and Allan Ahlberg (Puffin) and *Have You Seen My Duckling?* by Nancy Tafuri (Julia McRae).

One to three years

Sound, rhythm and rhyme are important to the one-year-old, as is the durability of books. Books need to be easily accessible and easily cleaned for this age group. It is best to explore simple themes relevant to the baby's life and then, as the child grows, to expand his knowledge to outside the house and into other environments. Tony Ross's *I Want My Potty* and *What's the Time Mr Wolf?* by P.D. Eastman (Collins) are two of my favourites. Other useful buys include *Big Wheels* and *Cars* both by Anne Rockwell (Hamish Hamilton). These clear and colourful books are especially useful for children who like cars and machinery of any kind. A series of books by Amanda Davidson entitled *Teddy at the Seaside*, *Teddy in the Garden*, and *Teddy's First Christmas* (Puffin) are delightful because children never seem to tire of teddy bears, no matter how old they are. Other Puffin favourites include *Peace at Last* by Jill Murphy. *Ten, Nine, Eight* by Molly Bang, *My Cat Likes to Hide in Boxes* by Eve Sutton and Lynley Dodd and *Captain Pugwash* by John Ryan.

Three to five years

The three-year-old is usually keen to explore the wider world and enjoys books involving funny situations and funny illustrations. By this age I have found that children are already showing distinct preferences when it comes to choosing books to read and indeed make their needs very clear when it comes to how the book is to be read. From cover to cover thank you, and no stopping in between. Bedtime stories are a great habit to get into at this point. You will be laying the groundwork for a lifetime of enjoyment by making the time to read your child a story each night.

Many lovely books exist for this age group including the beautifully illustrated *Alfie* series by Shirley Hughes (Collins). These include *Alfie Gives a Hand, Alfie's Feet* and *Alfie Gets in First.* The *Mog* series by Judith Kerr (Collins) includes *Mog the Forgetful Cat, Mog and the Baby* and *Mog in the Dark.* Other favourites include *Time to Get Out of the Bath, Shirley* by John Burningham (Collins), *The Trouble With Mum* by Babette Cole (Collins) and Bob Graham's *Libby, Oscar and Me* (Collins).

Five to eight years

Children who are beginning to read for themselves need short stories that are well worth the effort. Many children will want to return to old favourites, including picture books, and I don't see any reason why they shouldn't. Each child develops at his own pace and the significant point is that he wants to read something, anything. Most poor readers that I've met don't like to read, so we need to get children 'hooked' early in life and encourage them to develop their reading skills and their maturing tastes in reading matter with time and patience. *Katie Morag Delivers the Mail* (Collins) by Mairi Hedderwick heads my list of favourites. Pat Ross's *M and M Series* (Collins) about the adventures of best friends Mimi and Mandy is another firm favourite (Collins). *Avocado Baby* by John Burningham (Picture Lions) is hysterically funny. *Ernest and Celestine* by Gabrielle (Picture Lions) is a beautiful exploration of the relationship between a lumbering bear and a tiny mouse.

I have found that the above-mentioned books are enjoyed just as much by the parents as the children: the sign of a truly successful book. Some books for the older set include the Collins publications *Chips and Jessie* by Shirley Hughes, *The Peopling of Australia* by Percy Trezise, *When the Wind Changed* by Ruth Park and *Mulga Bill's Bicycle* by Banjo Paterson.

Organisations

Australian Association of Speech and Hearing

212 Clarendon St, East Melbourne, Victoria, 3002

This is the professional association of speech pathologists in Australia. It has details about most aspects relating to speech pathology and its services throughout Australia. It can provide you with a detailed list of practitioners as well as information regarding minimal fees for assessment and treatment.

Australian Government NAL Hearing Services Program

See your telephone book in the Commonwealth Government section

These centres assess, free of charge, hearing for those people under twenty-one years of age. They also supply hearing aids.

Community Health Centres

See your telephone book in the Commonwealth Government section

These centres offer a wide range of community services including psychology, family counselling, hearing testing and speech pathology. Not all centres offer the same services.

Private Speech Pathologists Association of New South Wales

104 Norman Ave, Thornleigh, New South Wales, 2120

This association has information regarding all aspects of private speech pathology practice and treatment.

Public Hospitals

See the listing under Hospitals in the telephone book

Most public hospitals have an audiology department where you child's hearing can be assessed free of charge.

INDEX

Acknowledgements

Thank you to: Kirsty Melville for her enthusiastic support; Elenie Poulos for her interest and editing skills; Roger Roberts for his humorous illustrations; and all my patients over the years who have provided me with a neverending source of knowledge. And to my family for their constant interest in all that I do.